COLLEGE 101

A Girl's Guide to
Freshman Year

MAR. 19

Top Advice From a Girl Who Just Went Through It!

COLLEGE 101

A Girl's Guide to Freshman Year

Julie Zeilinger

PRUFROCK PRESS INC.
WACO, TEXAS

CHAPTER 1

WHAT COLLEGE IS REALLY LIKE

Congratulations—you've made it to the first page of this book which means you're soon going to college (or presumably at least have some kind of vague interest in college). Either way, before we go any further I think I should be very clear: I'm not here to tell you that college is going to be the best 4 years of your life. In fact, I disagree with that wildly popular myth. I really don't think college will be the Best Experience of Your Life. In fact, I sincerely hope it's not.

That being said, I understand the impulse to glorify the undergraduate experience. Even if the very act of going to college is a financial burden (and, believe me, we will discuss that in greater depth—I have some capital F Feelings about the student loan disaster situation), a lot of people make the case that it's basically the ultimate sweet spot: You have enough freedom to make your own decisions and to have a ton of fun whenever you want, but not so much freedom that you have to worry about adult responsibilities like paying bills or taxes. Your job is to learn, to have fun, to *discover yourself* (in terms of your mind *and* body, if you catch my drift). And it's still socially acceptable to eat like a truck driver who has given up on life, and drink at otherwise wildly inappropriate times (read: at literally any time)! And, really, is that not the very definition of perfect happiness (especially when I frame it that way)?

Here's the thing, though: *College isn't really like that.*

Well, okay, it is like that in a superficial way. Most myths about college are true on some level and I don't want to paint a picture of college as akin to a Dickensian orphanage—you do discover new things about yourself, have plenty of fun, and even learn a thing or two. But the depiction of college as a manic experience of free love and nonstop partying only scrapes the surface of what college is really like. Like most things in life, college is full of highs *and* lows, full of experiences that aren't necessarily good or bad. And yet, we're all pretty dedicated to maintaining a culture of silence about our struggles, about bolstering the myth that college is a giant, equalizing party when the freshman year experience can also be isolating, difficult, and even downright scary.

The thing is, if we were all more transparent about our struggles as freshmen (and beyond), we would find we all feel the same way—which would probably make everybody feel *a lot* better. Openness and honesty don't erase difficult experiences, but they can make them a little easier to navigate to one's advantage—especially as women. We need to be honest about college and present it as an experience that's nuanced, that's full of all kinds of emotional, psychological, and academic experiences that *are* different for women.

Enter this book. Drawing from my own experience, the experiences of college-aged women who just went through this process, and various experts, I hope to debunk most of these myths, big and small, so that you don't have to reinvent the wheel and instead can embrace and learn from the experiences of those who have already been there. Basically, I'm going to give you all the advice, tips, and facts I wish I had back in 2011 when—bright-eyed and bushy-tailed—I first stepped foot on campus.

I'll tell you the truth about everything from what to expect in the classroom (how to get ahead . . . and, yes, when to take a step back) and (mostly) what to expect outside of it. We'll discuss room-mates (God help us all), relationships (they still exist, kind of!), hooking up and sex (and none of that vague, wishy-washy advice—the *real* stuff), as well as more serious (yet very real and pervasive) issues like sexual health and violence. We'll even talk about debt, but not in an economic, droning way: in the straightforward need-to-know, this-is-how-we-can-avoid-getting-screwed-over way. And those are just the highlights.

But before we get into the details, I'd like to take a look at the big picture and debunk the biggest, overarching myths of all.

> **MYTH:** Adapting to college is not a big deal—after orientation you're totally set, and if you're not having the most fun ever all the time, then you're doing it wrong.
>
> **TRUTH:** Freshman year can be a real bitch.

I (like most other newbies) went off to college my freshman year under the impression that I was headed toward the greatest experience of my life. Hastily constructed college movies full of crappy dialogue and 30-year-old actors with perfect faces and bodies cast as 18-year-old freshmen had completely swayed my idea of what to expect, leading me to believe that instead of a liberal arts school in Manhattan, I was actually bound for some version of an orgy interspersed with classes like "The Sociological Impact of Mercantilism in Western Europe: 1600–1750" (you know, prac-tical, useful information that would directly impact and inform a later career). But I soon found that, despite having talked with plenty of current college students and having attended a relatively academically rigorous high school *and* reading guidebooks, I was unprepared. Beyond increased academic difficulty or new social situations, I was hardly prepared for even the most basic experience of *existing* at college in a structural way.

It didn't take too long after stepping on campus to basically have a panic attack. I was convinced that I was failing at life and began—to my abject horror—to long for my high school days. I hardly graduated high school as the Prom Queen beloved by the student body, whom teachers tearily hugged good-bye, wondering if they should abdicate their professions having perfected the student-teacher relationship with me. (I was—not entirely inaccurately—known as the weirdo with a dark sense of humor. C'est la vie.)

But it soon became painfully evident how, despite being a confusing time of self-discovery and growing pains (to put it mildly), high school is also undeniably straightforward. High school is highly segmented and chronological, dictated by deadlines and schedules. You go to school for 6 or 7 hours a day, 5 days a week, week in and week out. The impressive consistency of this framework is diversified by notable events like Homecoming and Prom (and all that other social crap that seems like a Really Big Deal at the time but, in retrospect, will seem relatively insignificant, I promise), academic benchmarks like regular quizzes and tests, and the glorious paradises that are high school summers. A student's high school experience is laid out before her and defined by concrete indicators of progress either achieved or failed.

Dealing with college on the most basic level of existence is kind of a free for all. There's plenty of work—midterms, finals, papers, and lab reports abound (rejoice!)—but basically your time is completely your own beyond the relatively few hours you spend in the classroom. Your schedule—and life—is an open book. Nobody at college—professors or fellow students alike—will check up on or in with you. Your parents may be only a motivational and encouraging phone call away, but a phone call is different than the type of monitoring that probably used to incite endless eye-rolls and under-the-breath muttering in high school. You're on your own.

Most high school students look forward to this kind of freedom. And it's true: There are no curfews, no seemingly arbitrary rules, and, I won't lie, it's a limitlessness that can be incredibly empowering and plain awesome. But it's also easy for everything from how you should pragmatically spend your time to your overall purpose and life direction to become less clear without those benchmarks and segmented, prescribed time. It's a complex experience and one that can be deceptively challenging to navigate.

So if college isn't *entirely* fun and games then why are we so committed to projecting such an idealistic version of the experience? I think it starts at the very beginning of the college application process—especially when it comes to the idea of "fit" or that there is a single institution that's perfect for each prospective student. At some point during the past few decades, the whole college process became a veritable romantic comedy starring you (a terrified and/or somewhat apathetic high school student more concerned with passing the SATs than with the typical leading lady dilemma of saving your struggling cupcake bakery or boutique dog grooming shop) and the decades old Ivy-covered campus that is Your Perfect Fit (which is less a macho-yet-sensitive love interest than it is an inanimate object with a history of misogyny and institutional exclusion). The myth continues once you step foot on campus: You're supposed to lay your eyes on the University of Your Dreams (your Sexy Love Interest) and *know* that it just feels *right* and that you *belong*.

Here's the thing. This romantic narrative is far too black and white and (much like real rom-coms) wildly unrealistic. In this version of the story, there is one college that is Right For You that will ensure Perfect Happiness and a Great Future. But in reality, colleges are not fairytale resorts designed to hand students happiness and success in exchange for their tuition (although, based on tuition rates, it's not unreasonable to expect that that would be the case). Rather, the "college experience" is intimately shaped by who ends up attending the same school (and of those people, who ends up on your hall freshman year, who also writes for the school paper, etc.), which classes you get into, and which professors deign to enlighten the minds of undergraduates that semester. Your college experience is going to be less about this mythic idea of "fit," less about the right college providing you with everything you need and leading you along a guided journey (like the prescribed high school experience), than it is going to be what *you* do with basic resources made available to you and the mindset with which you approach them. Ultimately, college is a dynamic experience in which *you are half the equation* and a hugely informative source of your own experience. It's not up to the college to hand you a great experience: You have to navigate your newfound freedom and fight for your own happiness.

> **MYTH:** If you are struggling, you're the only one who is.
> **TRUTH:** *Everybody* goes through a period of adjustment—there's just a weird culture of silence about maintaining the aforementioned idealistic illusions about college.

It took years for the truth about our freshman years to come out among my friends. During one ~~study session~~ Buzzfeed-trolling marathon my sophomore year, some friends and I started reminiscing about the previous year. One friend got straight to the point: "Did you guys also feel terrified and unprepared basically all the time? Or was that just me?" The entire group immediately erupted into a chorus of "Oh my god, yes" and "I definitely thought I was the only one failing at life." We had all assumed we were the only ones who felt unprepared for a radically new and different experience, that we were completely alone in our social and academic struggles, and yet it wasn't until after the fact that we realized we had all had the same freshman experience—one that is probably far more common than not.

So why are we so committed to this silence? Well, the Hunger Games-Sparta-fight-to-the-death hybrid that is the college admissions process certainly sets the tone for how we approach the entire experience. The independence, ruthless determination, and single-minded competition the process requires breed isolation: We know there are only a limited number of spots, finite opportunities in college admissions and beyond. We get into a pattern of withholding information, of refusing to lend a helping hand that extends far beyond the college process. It's every woman for herself.

It's an attitude that's specifically ingrained in women beyond college, too: We're entering into a workplace that still undeniably breeds gender discrimination. Women in the workplace are routinely pegged for the mommy-track and passed over for promotions and leadership opportunities and are subject to sexual harassment and other race- and gender-based discrimination (Catalyst, 2012). Consciously or not, many young women have watched their mothers and have deduced that the workplace (and, in many ways, society at large) is still not open to women the way it is to men. But instead of attacking the sexist system that produces such attitudes, women attack and compete against each other for those limited spots. This understanding of female-based competition may be more subconscious than not (as admittedly few of us have directly experienced such workplace dynamics as high school students), but the cultural attitude permeates us: Instead of drawing strength from each other and learning from each other's mistakes, we continuously repeat them based on the idea that we must selfishly guard our own experiences because success for women is a limited resource. We make things unnecessarily difficult for ourselves and allow that power dynamic to persist.

It also doesn't help that young women are pressured to be perfect, to never admit to any kind of failure, in a way that young men simply are not. Starting as early as middle and high school but continuing and even intensifying in college, we're brainwashed to believe that we have to do really well in school, meet narrow

CHAPTER 2

PREPARING FOR D-DAY

Getting Ready for Freshman Year (And How to Deal When It Actually Happens)

One of the strongest memories I have from the summer before I left for college was cleaning out a closet full of about a decade's worth of accumulated junk. I think it took me the better part of a week to sort through an impressive array of stuffed animals, various trophies of participation given to all of the equally untalented athletes on my various elementary school teams, and every greeting card I'd ever been given (I may or may not be a hoarder, jury's still out).

To any other normal human being at any other time in her life, that hodgepodge of random items would be all but meaningless, but to my sentimental, nostalgic, recent high school graduate self, every single item evoked an emotionally charged memory. At some point, I ended up crumpled on my bedroom floor in despair, clutching a birthday card created on Microsoft Word 1998 in Comic Sans font (vital details: every word was a different color and the paper bordered with irrelevant clip art). "Marissa wrote me this for my 10th birthday," I sobbed, referring to what was obviously a hastily assembled birthday card from my best friend. "I WILL

NEVER FIND ANOTHER FRIEND WHO UNDERSTANDS ME EVER AGAIN!"

That may have been an emotional low point of the summer, but the fact remains: Even if the product of 90's-era cutting edge technology doesn't exactly inspire sobbing, the months that hang between high school and college are seriously challenging. Some people feel like they should ready themselves for a new chapter by pulling away from their high school friends. Others experience extreme nostalgia and are more willing to forgive any negative memories about their childhood and high school in favor of an idealized view of the past. And then there's the strong contingent who hated their high school, hometown, and everything associated with both and are methodically counting down the days until they can escape. No matter how you feel, the bottom line is that being in a state of in between, in a drawn-out transition, is incredibly difficult.

And at the same time that you're dealing with all of those feelings, there's the very concrete reality of actually, physically getting ready for college. You're going to be on your own for the first time and trying to anticipate what you'll need (not to mention what you'll *want*) as you break out on your own can be tricky.

But not to fear: As somebody who showed up to school with everything she didn't need (three umbrellas and more power strips than there were outlets in the room) and sans some essentials (remembering to bring a laundry bag probably would've been a good idea), I've got hindsight on my side. By the end of this chapter you'll be so prepared for this transition that your RA will probably (gladly) recruit you to lead your first floor meeting.

CONNECTING WITH OTHER STUDENTS

Even before you pack, one of the first things you'll likely do after enrolling in school is to join the freshman class's Facebook page. Part of being a member of this brave new digital world is accepting the fact that the very existence of major life events is questionable if they're not documented on some form of social media platform. We're all expected to record every aspect of our existence, from the miniscule to the milestones.

But joining your class's Facebook group is actually an excellent way to get a sense of who will surround you on a daily basis. Although for the most part you should approach the whole thing with an open mind by commenting and posting when you feel moved to do so and enjoying/observing others' posts, here are some key points to remember.

DON'T BE THAT KID

Almost without fail, there is usually one kid who manages to single themselves out on these Facebook pages—even on pages with thousands of students. On my class's page, it was a girl who thought it was a good idea to post multiple videos of her rants about the patriarchy . . . to a group of complete strangers. The "that kid" of a friend's class Facebook group was a guy who would post links to highly pretentious thought pieces then pick fights with anybody who dared to disagree with his (extensively detailed) opinions about them. Just remember that this is the very first impression your *entire* class will have of you—and it's amazing how, although most students can barely remember what their professor said 5 minutes ago, even as seniors *everybody* remembers the kid who dominated their class's Facebook page the summer before freshman year.

DON'T BE AFRAID TO POST, EITHER

That being said, this *is* your first chance to get to know your future fellow classmates. Although you probably shouldn't try to dominate the page or let your freak flag fly (wait until finals when the full range of human and even animal behavior is not just acceptable but expected), it's actually a good idea to reach out. Introduce yourself, mention some of the things you're passionate about, ask if somebody wants to attend a nearby concert that fall—whatever you choose to write, just make yourself known. Finding somebody who shares an interest by reaching out to everybody all at once is far more efficient than engaging in a ton of individual conversations. I know of people who found great friends due to a shared interest expressed on their class's Facebook page—people they may not have encountered otherwise. Also, it's great to show up on campus with a plan to meet up with some people or to look out for somewhat familiar faces—it makes the transition that much easier. Just make sure you don't greet people like you know them if you're only acquainted with them by surreptitiously viewing their profile without any real contact. It's an easy trap to fall into but a very, very creepy one.

DON'T JUDGE OTHERS BY THEIR POSTS

I think it's a pretty well-established fact at this point that people more often than not present themselves differently on the Internet than they do in person. Especially when introducing themselves to a ton of potential friends, kids often self-consciously rewrite their posts multiple times until their true voice and thoughts are unrecognizable (or, conversely, don't think *enough* about how they're coming off to a ton of different people; i.e., "That Kid"). Don't allow a single Facebook post to completely shape your view of an individual: Try to give him or her the benefit of the doubt.

RAIDING BED, BATH & BEYOND: WHAT DO I BRING?

There is one very basic rule you need to remember when packing for college: Do not—I repeat, do *not*—bring every worldly possession with you to school. In fact, you should bring the absolute minimal amount of material possessions possible. Although your first instinct might be to bring along things that remind you of home and offer some kind of comfort and familiarity, you may feel differently when you show up to your tiny dorm room. The truth is, being able to walk around your clutter-free room will be far more comforting than climbing over nonessential possessions that remind you of home.

But what qualifies as essential? Of course, it's ultimately up to you to know what you really need (and want) at school, but Figure 1 provides some basic guidelines.

WHAT TO PACK

1. Bedding
- **Bedsheets, Blankets, a Comforter, Pillow, and Pillowcase:** Thanks to almost every college's insistence on providing *extra-long* twin beds, which NOBODY ELSE EVER IN THE WORLD has, you likely won't be able to bring your own bedding because that would make too much sense.
- **A Mattress Pad:** Arguably less essential but it actually makes a *huge* difference. They're not exactly cheap, but my roommate's mattress pad-less bed felt like a wooden plank compared to my luxuriously soft and comfortable sleeping arrangement. And in college, getting a good night's sleep is *always* a solid investment.

2. Room
- **Desk and/or Floor Lamp:** If you're like me, fluorescent lights—the dorm room light of choice—act quicker than any kind of downer in pill form possibly could. Invest in soft/soothing/human-friendly lighting instead.
- **Alarm Clock:** A smartphone's alarm works just fine, but in case you want to double up on alarms before a final.
- **Power Strips:** There are never enough outlets. NEVER.
- **Kitchen Supplies:** Including plastic plates and dishware, nonperishable food like granola bars and, for the real food-lovers out there, a mini fridge.

3. Toiletries
- **Towels:** Of the bath, wash, and hand variety.
- **Robe:** Unless you want to parade around in just a towel, then go ahead.
- **Hair Supplies:** Hair dryers/straighteners/curlers are handy.
- **Shower Caddy:** Full of the basics—shampoo, conditioner, you hopefully know the hygiene drill by now.
- **Shower Flip Flops:** Arguably the most essential thing for facing a communal, questionably sanitary shower.
- **Over-the-Counter and/or Prescription Meds:** Advil/Tylenol, cough drops, decongestants, Pepto Bismol—you will need all of them at some point, trust me.
- **First Aid Kit:** Including bandages, antiseptic cream, etc.—college is a war zone.

4. Technology
- **Laptop:** You likely already have one, but if you used your high school's computer lab or shared a family computer, seriously consider investing in a laptop. Although most schools have communal computer labs, laptops can be great for taking notes in class, writing papers, and access to endless mindless distractions. Many online marketplaces and even big name stores offer student discounts.

FIGURE 1. WHAT TO PACK FOR YOUR DORM ROOM.

- **Chargers (for Phone and Laptop):** If you have extras, bring those too.
- **Printer:** Most schools have printers available for students' use, but if you're a procrastinator who likes to print out papers without waiting in line or worrying about technical difficulties 5 minutes before class, consider bringing your own.
- **USB Flash Drive:** BACK UP EVERYTHING. EVERYTHING. You never know when your computer will just up and die on you, but you can probably count on it happening at some *super* convenient time, like in the middle of finals because *of course* that would happen.

5. Clothing
- **Winter/Seasonal Clothes:** Coat, gloves, hat, winter boots if applicable.
- **Fancy Clothes:** Especially if you're planning on rushing a sorority, you'll need a dress for formal and other recruitment events.
- **Business Attire:** Your school will likely have a career fair or other professional events—don't show up in sweats. You're a semi-adult now, dammit.
- **Everyday Clothes:** Jeans and T-shirts are your friends.
- **Pajamas:** These double as everyday clothes after those first few weeks when you're no longer trying.
- **Shoes:** Less is more; generally you'll need athletic shoes, a good pair of heels, a nice pair of flats, sandals, and boots.
- **Bags:** Wristlets are always great for going out; bigger shoulder bags are great for carrying notebooks/books to class.
- **Jewelry:** Just don't bring anything too valuable.
- **Swimsuit:** If you like to do laps or if you go to a warm-climate school . . . lucky.
- **Workout Clothes:** Exercise is a *huge* stress release and is also pretty good for you . . . or so I'm told.
- **Sewing Kit:** For when you inevitably destroy something. It happens.
- **Laundry Supplies:** Hangers, detergent, laundry bag, stain removers like Tide To-Go Pens, which are akin to a religious experience, I swear, and Downy wrinkle releaser or an iron/ironing board if you're old school.

6. School Supplies
- **Note-Taking Supplies:** If you don't plan to take notes on your computer, make sure you have the basics, including:
  - **Notebooks and Pens/Pencils:** Reacquaint yourself with your handwriting and give your prematurely arthritic fingers a break from typing.
  - **Sticky Notes:** These are so useful for studying, writing yourself reminders, or writing your sleeping roommate a note and leaving it on her forehead (LOL COLLEGE IS FUN!).
  - **Paper Clips, a Stapler, Scissors:** Basically any stationery material you feel you objectively don't need in the digital age but then *always* end up needing.

FIGURE 1. CONTINUED.

- **Calculator:** May the quantitative forces be with you.
- **Folders:** Organization is key. Keep track of various handouts, readings, and returned papers and you'll be that much more prepared for finals—seriously, it makes a difference.

7. Miscellaneous Stuff
- **Important Papers:** Bank info, car registration, financial aid forms.
- **Important Cards**: Driver's license, credit cards, medical insurance card, Social Security card.
- **Dorm Survival Aids:** Earplugs (for when you have a 9 a.m. exam and your roommate does not), fan, flashlight, a duffel/overnight bag (for when you need to escape).
- **Umbrella:** Try to keep a small one with you in your bag—you *will* get caught in the rain when you're having an awesome hair day.
- **Beach Towels:** For sunbathing when you should be studying, plus for dealing with any number of disgusting dorm-related situations, just trust me.

FIGURE 1. CONTINUED.

A DIFFERENT KIND OF "GIRLS GONE WILD": THE ROOMMATE

THE ROOMMATE ASSIGNMENT

Different schools handle the roommate assignment differently. Many allow you to request a roommate, most have the option of random matching, and some still require that you show up on move-in day without a clue about who will already be unpacking their stuff in your room. If you do have the option to choose whether or not you want to pick your own roommate or undergo a random assignment, there are some pros and cons to consider, as noted in Table 1.

Table 1
The Roommate Assignment

	PROS	CONS
CHOOSING YOUR ROOMMATE	There's a degree of comfort—whether you choose to live with a friend from home or somebody you met at a new students weekend or on the Facebook group, you probably know at least some defining details about the person with whom you'll be sharing a room for a year. You can also coordinate purchases for the room, like a mini-fridge (you know, the truly important things).	Especially if you choose to live with a close friend, you may be relegating yourself to your comfort zone *too* much. Although it's totally possible to branch out with your best friend at your side, feeling like you have to be the same person you've always been with her may make it hard to explore other aspects of yourself. Also, spending social *and* down time with your best friend is a *lot* of time together. Chances are you'll begin to irritate each other and the lack of space could actually harm your relationship. On the other hand, if you choose to live with somebody you have only met a few times or have only talked to online and are basing that decision off of a few interactions, random selection may actually be the better way to go. The school will likely base their assignment off of some concrete preferences (like wake-up time or study preferences) rather than an impression.
RANDOM SELECTION	Like I pointed out above, chances are your school is working off of some kind of survey you filled out, so you will likely have at least some lifestyle-based preferences in common with your roommate. As you'll find out, this may be more valuable than having actual interests in common: At the end of the day you want to be comfortable and at peace in the place you live, not committed to a 24/7 sleepover.	You (and frankly, the people assigning you to your roommate) have no idea what this girl is actually like. She could present herself one way on paper and turn out to be completely different. You just never know what you're going to get.

WHAT TO EXPECT WHEN YOU'RE EXPECTING . . . A ROOMMATE

I suspect that it is a universal (and perverse) hobby of college upperclassmen and graduates alike to terrify rising freshman with cautionary roommate stories of horror. The summer before my freshman year, it seemed like all I had to do was mention the fact that I was about to start college and aforementioned upperclassmen/graduates would inquire about my roommate situation. Apparently, admitting that I didn't yet know my roommate was basically an invitation to terrify me with stories of the ill-adjusted human beings assigned to live with whomever I might have been talking to. So, believe me, I was prepared for the worst.

I am happy to report that I did *not* get stuck with a sociopath. I never woke up to my roommate hovering above my bed, whispering, "I just like watching you sleep." My roommate never horded insect-attracting stashes of food, didn't attempt to build a replica of Mount Everest out of her laundry, and never required me to dismiss "very special" visitors. We were never best friends, but we respected each other's space and requests, asked about each other's days, and occasionally shared amusing anecdotes.

I'll admit, I was like many other rising freshmen girls: I definitely had an idealized vision of my roommate relationship. I imagined long nights of plotting future world domination over jars of Nutella, living together every year, and then post-graduation making time for weekly power brunches despite our busy schedules dominating our respective fields. That definitely didn't happen, but in retrospect I consider myself pretty lucky. One of the most astonishing and almost impressive things I remember from my freshman year were the stories of other people's roommates who somehow made it through 18 years of life without getting some basic memos about how humans interact with each other.

As it turns out, having a courteous, respectful, and somewhat professional relationship with your roommate may actually be the ideal living situation. Friends of mine who were instantaneous best friends with their roommates often ended up fighting with them, their relationship strained by *constant* exposure to each other. Constant interaction with *anybody*, even somebody you really like and care about, is a lot of work.

The Actual Rules You and Your Roommate Should Use to Make a Contract

Many RAs will require that you and your roommate make a formal contract that outlines your ground rules for living together. Even if it's not required, though, it's *absolutely* a good idea to create some kind of agreement anyway. You'll definitely want something concrete to refer to if you and your roommate(s) get into some kind of argument or situation. Don't be afraid to be brutally honest and to advocate for your own comfort: The standard questions about keeping the room clean and whether or not you're a night owl or early riser probably won't cut it. Here are some rules you might want to throw out there:

1. If you're in a long-distance relationship, please avoid marathon Skype sessions (or phone or Skype sex) that last well into the early morning hours.
2. If you do have a boyfriend or girlfriend, please give me some notice if you plan on sexiling (exiling a roommate for the purpose of sex) me—*especially* if they are visiting for *multiple days.*
3. If you get back really late or get up really early and I'm asleep, please make *every effort* to be as quiet as possible.
4. Don't. Eat. My. Food.
5. Please engage in any and all illegal activity outside of the room (including drugs, alcohol, or the selling of either).
6. Rooms/suites should generally be clean. Let's figure out some type of chore wheel or fair way to address that.
7. You also need to clean yourself. If your body odor is the dominant scent in our living space, we have a problem.

The most common types of challenging roommates. And of course, there are the roommates who necessitate some serious character building. For dealing with *those* roommates, I can offer some advice.

TYPE 1
The Anti-Social or Socially Awkward

I HAVE TOO MUCH WORK TO HANG OUT!

The situation. Whether it's because she has mistaken your room for the library and studies 24/7 or because she's possibly agoraphobic, this roommate always gives you a hard time about having people over and never allows you any privacy. It's easy to roll your eyes at this roommate, complain about her to other friends, and label her a weirdo, but there are plenty of very serious possible reasons driving her antisocial behavior. She may be putting so much pressure on herself to succeed academically that she can't handle being social, she may be painfully shy or even depressed—"weird" shouldn't be the go-to assumption.

The solution. Reach out to her. It may feel counterintuitive if her rules and general presence are pissing you off, but oftentimes, the people who reject social interaction are the ones who need friends the most. Try to get to the bottom of why she's so opposed to socializing (in a noninvasive, respectful way, of course). If that doesn't work, just accept that she is who she is and try to respect her wishes. Definitely don't speak badly about her behind her back or alienate her further.

TYPE 2
The Mean Girl

The situation. This roommate didn't get the memo that high school ended and thinks it's still permissible to make immature comments and be manipulative. Maybe she'll make a comment about how the Freshman 15 really affects *some* people more than others. Maybe she'll silently judge your outfits. She makes your room into a passive or blatantly aggressive war zone.

The solution. It's never easy to rise above somebody's horrible behavior, especially if it's directed at you, but it's necessary to try. At the risk of sounding like your mother when you were in middle school, try talking it out. Be honest about how she's making you feel, ask her why she's behaving this way, and ask her to stop (like good adults are supposed to). If that doesn't work, just try to be unfailingly nice to her despite her rudeness. Mean girls thrive on evoking reactions from their victims: She wants to get in a war with you because she feeds off the drama, but you won't benefit from a fight; you'll just waste time and energy. Don't give in, but talk to your RA (resident assistant) if things get really bad. If it's a truly unbearable situation, look into your school's room change policy.

TYPE 3

The "Slut"

The situation. First of all, it's really crappy to refer to other girls as "sluts"—to make judgments about them based on their sexual practices and/or preferences. It's a sexist double standard to view women negatively for expressing themselves sexually in a way that men are encouraged to. Women aren't doing themselves any favors by perpetuating these standards by holding each other to ridiculous standards of "purity."

Can you find **somewhere** else to sleep tonight?

That being said, it's one thing to support a woman's right to sleep with whomever she wants, whenever she wants generally, and another to have to live in the place where she's doing that. You have a right to privacy and, beyond that, a right not to be greatly inconvenienced by her sexual exploration.

The solution. Again, don't call your roommate or anybody else a "slut" behind her back (or to her face, for that matter). It can be tempting to gossip about your roommate, especially when it's so encouraged in our culture and especially if her behavior is making you uncomfortable or is annoying. Resist. Accept that if it does seem like she's genuinely having a good time sexually experimenting and liberating herself, that that is just a part of college for many women. However, it's also worth noting that if you get the sense that your roommate is being so sexually active out of insecurity, to prove something to herself, or for any other negative reasons, then you should try talking to her about it. Talking through her issues may prove to be a much more helpful coping mechanism for any type of trauma or other issues she might be trying to navigate.

But, as for you: You have a right to set boundaries (and the earlier you do so, the better). It can be awkward to talk about sex—especially with somebody you just met—but it's important to take a firm stance on hook up rules right away for the sake of your long-term comfort. Write up a contract and don't be afraid to confront her if she breaches it.

TYPE 4
The Thief/Mooch

The situation. It's beyond obnoxious to come back to your room to find your stuff moved, missing, or broken. Beyond being incredibly frustrating and inconvenient, it's really unsettling to feel insecure about the safety of your possessions and to always feel like you have to be alert in what should be a safe, comforting space.

The solution. First and foremost, make it clear whether or not she can have access to your stuff on the first day of school. If for whatever reason you didn't discuss those boundaries, you need to confront her as soon as you suspect she may be using or taking your things. I'm always surprised by how many girls, afraid of conflict, notice their stuff is missing but refuse to confront their roommate about it. Of course, accusing somebody of being a thief is no small matter and shouldn't be done haphazardly, but if you're pretty sure your roommate is to blame you *need* to talk to her. There's obviously an ideal way to do this, and it's not to confront her as soon as she walks in the door and shout "THIEF! BEHEAD HER!" to your invisible army of enraged village people. First, ask if she "borrowed" your possessions. If she admits it, clearly request that she ask for permission to do so the next time or make it clear that your stuff is off limits. If she denies it, try to trust that she didn't but if it's a reoccurring situation, present her with the evidence for your suspicions and lay down the law. If this pattern persists, get your RA involved. Although it would really suck to have to do this, if the situation does not abate, you may want to consider locking up your valuable stuff or switching rooms. The same basic situation applies to mooches: If they're not stealing your stuff, but borrowing a lot of your stuff or generally relying on you for food or anything else, make it clear that true friendships are based on respect and reciprocation, and that by mooching off of you, they're not demonstrating either.

TYPE 5
The Nonexistent Roommate

I'll see you when I see you!

The situation. Especially if you don't get along, this situation can seem like a blessing at first: Your roommate is never around and it basically feels like you have your own room—sweet freedom! But ultimately, if you have no idea where your roommate disappears to, it can be really disconcerting: Every time she disappears you have no idea if it's because she's staying with a friend, out of town, or lying in a ditch somewhere. Even if you're not close, you feel like you have some kind of obligation to alert somebody if she goes missing . . . but don't want to overreact. It's a difficult balance.

The solution. When she does reappear, make sure everything is okay and, if you think it will make you feel better, ask her to at least check in with a text letting you know she's alive. Beyond that, invest yourself in other things and be thankful you essentially ended up with a single at the double rate. If you start to get lonely, don't be afraid to keep your door open (if you live on a hall in a dorm) or to invite friends over to hang out in your room or to keep each other company while you work.

I think the bottom line is this: Whether you love or hate your roommate, having one at all will be a valuable life experience. Learning to live with somebody who is basically a complete stranger inevitably teaches you so much about yourself. You learn your limits and the boundaries of your patience, sure, but also self-awareness and the ability to compromise (ideally). At the very least, you get a few interesting stories out of it.

THAT DORM LIFE GRIND

I probably don't have to explicitly state this, but living in a dorm/any type of communal living situation at college is *a lot* different than living at home. I'm not sure which was more disappointing: Finding out that the tooth fairy is a giant conspiracy perpetuated with an almost impressive dedication by the adult world, or finding that there isn't a dorm fairy—that moving out really means you're living on your own. If your mom never made you do your own laundry, picked up after you, and nursed you back

DORMCEST

"Dormcest" refers to hooking up with somebody who also lives in your dorm. As a proud lazy woman, I have to say that the convenience and accessibility of this arrangement does make it an understandably enticing option. However, there are some considerable downsides. If things don't go well (which, let's be honest, 9 times out of 10 is the case), then it can make for an incredibly uncomfortable living situation, which just sucks. There's ample potential for awkward run-ins, blatant hostility, and even the possibility of running into your hook-up with their new partner—and that's just scraping the surface. Your room and dorm generally should be a place of refuge where you feel most comfortable, not somewhere you feel you need to avoid or tread carefully.

My advice? Refrain from entering a romantic relationship with anybody in your dorm—in all cases, but *especially* if it's an intentionally casual relationship. Of course, if one of the residents of Room 525 makes your heart flutter, your knees weak, and shares your passion for artisanal jam making—go for it. I'm all for true love and after all, you're a big girl and you can make your own decisions. Just beware that although relatively common, hooking up with somebody in your dorm has a high potential for making your life way more complicated than it has to be—and you already have bio homework for that.

MEAL PLANS

Many freshmen are required to be on a full meal plan for at least their first year. If that's the case, there's not a lot I can say except if the food is bad, suck it up—it's just a year. If it's good, definitely keep yourself in check. Your parents told you to eat your vegetables for a reason: If you only eat processed foods, you WILL BECOME ONE. Also, check out the chapter on wellness (Chapter 4) for tips about how to make nutritious choices on a meal plan (even in the most grease-soaked dining halls, it's possible to avoid becoming a moribund zombie, addicted to trans-fat and GMOs) and more on the weird dynamics of eating in college, especially as it relates to the way women tend to judge each other's food choices in really annoying and messed up ways.

It's also worth mentioning that dealing with the cafeteria dynamics required by being on a meal plan can feel a lot like being a high school freshman all over again. Before I left for college, I legitimately had nightmares about being the loner in the corner of the dining hall every single meal. In retrospect it seems ridiculous, but the idea of eating alone freaked me out and seemed like the epitome of social failure. In reality, nobody cares if you eat alone—everybody is really busy and most of the time if you want to eat, it's necessary to fly solo. Also, it can be kind of nice to have some alone time: In college, people surround you *all of the time*. It can be nice to have a few minutes of peace and quiet while you savor what may or may not be meatloaf.

LIFE HACKS

Laundry Edition

Even if you never had to do your own laundry before, there's no reason to be the person somehow covered in suds, staring at the washing machine like it's the safe you have to crack in the midst of a heist. Here are some tips:

- ◆ Leave baby powder on oil stains overnight—problem solved.
- ◆ Cover the edges of rips/runs in tights with clear nail polish to keep them from getting worse.
- ◆ Mix cold water and vinegar to scrub water stains off of leather.
- ◆ Spray sweat stains with lemon juice or rub them with a dryer sheet before you wash them.
- ◆ Shaving cream removes make-up from shirt collars.
- ◆ Did the string of your hoodie somehow get removed from the actual hood? Thread the string through a straw, then thread the straw through the holes.
- ◆ White wine removes red wine stains. You know, in case your 21+ friend asks you for wine stain removal tips.

But, if silent meals aren't for you, don't be afraid to ask to join a table. One of the great things about college is that it's *not* high school: Chances are you won't be judged or turned away, you'll just give yourself another opportunity to meet new people.

AND SO IT BEGINS ...
BEING FRESHMEAT

I'm going to give it to you straight: Upperclassmen generally find freshmen annoying. In most cases, this is not a hostile opposition or an active form of continuous hazing, but rather an impatience for their general newness. My personal theory is that awkward, confused, and generally terrified freshmen often evoke upperclassmen's memories of their own awkward and confused freshman terror, and they're too busy to deal with feelings, so they channel those feelings into antifreshmen sentiments. Or they're just jerks. It's definitely one of the two.

The best way to deal with these prevailing attitudes about freshmen is to first of all accept that they exist. They are unfair and often uncomfortable, but it's just generally how the hierarchy of college goes. Once you've accepted your relatively low status, own it. I don't mean belittle yourself or treat yourself like you are lesser than anybody else due solely to your age and newness. That's bullshit.

What I mean by accepting your position is don't posture—don't pretend like you're anything other than what you are. Be humble. Ask for help. Don't act like you have all of the answers. It may seem like acting like you already fit in will help you adapt, but I've found the opposite is actually true: People in general, as well as upperclassmen specifically, are much more amenable to those who are upfront about their shortcomings or about needing help rather than those who overcompensate.

However, you don't have to be completely clueless. It's amazing to me how little some college freshmen know when they step on campus when a lot of basic information—like where your classes are (get acquainted with a campus map, please) or the many functions of your student ID—is pretty easily accessible. Of course, it's not this kind of administrative information that rising freshmen are dying to know. It's the more subtle rules freshmen are usually clueless about: the emotions you'll have to navigate, the unspoken rules. That information is pretty hard to obtain from sources other than direct life experience and every campus has its own cultural intricacies. But luckily, you have this book. I can't tell you exactly what you'll feel and face and how to navigate it, but here are some hints.

(DIS)ORIENTATION: BEYOND THE "INFORMATION GUIDE"

I think the bottom line of college orientation is that it's all about the paradox of feeling simultaneously comforted and entirely thrown off your axis, spinning rapidly toward the unknown. Or at least, that's what orientation was like for me.

This paradox manifested itself at the very beginning of the "leaving-for-college-journey." After posting my obligatory, "Leaving for college. Thanks for the memories everybody!" Facebook status, I packed all of my earthly belongings into the family car. That's when I realized that all of my earthly belongings *fit into the family car.* Although the reality of this totally satisfied the fatalist in me (look how easy it would be for me to escape—so little materialistic baggage to weigh me down once the zombie apocalypse hits!), it also underscored the fact that the home I was leaving, the home I had grown up in and considered my own, really wasn't mine any more. Statements I had made with confidence ever since I clicked "submit" on my electronic application quickly turned to questions. This is what I want? I'm excited? I'm ready to be on my own?

But then I became immersed in Barnard's Orientation Program and got to know the campus and the incredible students that surrounded me. I felt somehow at peace, excited to start a new life. In fact, if I hadn't had to repeat my place of birth along with my name and intended major *every single time* I met somebody new, which was approximately every 5 minutes, I might even have temporarily forgotten about my home back in Ohio (but so it goes).

Here's the thing about orientation: It might seem like an innocuous series of events where the people running it unfailingly smile in a way that never reaches their eyes (the hallmark of all bureaucratically planned and funded events), but it can actually be pretty emotional. You'll likely feel any or all of these emotions.

Homesick. For some who have never been away from home for long, who may have never left their hometown before, just physically going to college can be a really big deal. Being in a new town, a different state, a completely unique subculture of the country can be a huge cultural adjustment for many people. It can be in small ways—a friend of mine from Arizona, for example, recalled complete bafflement about the boating shoes and cardigans that suddenly surrounded her when she arrived at Harvard—and in big ways, like feeling completely out of your element.

Even for those who have been away from home before, going to college can cause a unique type of homesickness. You know things will never be the same again: You'll just be visiting your childhood home, not living there (that is until after you graduate and can't get a job because of the crappy economy and need to move back in with your parents, but let's hope that doesn't happen). You begin to long not only for familiar physical surroundings but for that *feeling* of home: You long for the feeling of being taken care of as much as you wish you lived in a place that didn't feel like a clinical institution (linoleum, cinderblocks, unidentifiable stains, and all).

Feeling homesick is totally and completely normal. Although at first it may feel like it will last forever, homesickness *will* subside. You'll soon be so busy—with school, with new friends, with new opportunities—that you'll forget to miss home. And after some more time passes, school will even start to feel like home.

Euphoric. For extroverts, orientation will probably be a spectacular experience. You get to talk about yourself endlessly without seeming narcissistic, and it's one of the few times where social norms are acceptably suspended. How many times in life can you simply plunk yourself down at a table full of perfect strangers and put minimal effort into justifying your presence (a quip is preferable, but even "Chicken fingers are delicious. Am I right or am I right?" will suffice). Your peers, paralyzed by fear and the sheer newness of the situation might silently judge you and make mental notes, but externally they'll accept you. There are endless opportunities to meet *all* of the new people. Extroverts, this is your moment to shine. Enjoy.

Lonely. For all of the introverts out there (like me), orientation can be a really lonely, exhausting experience. The majority of the conversations you'll have during orientation will inevitably be superficial. When you're used to the kind of easy interactions that come from years of being around the same general group of people, who understand (and accept) your quirks or even just have a working knowledge of your likes and dislikes, it can be really challenging to start from scratch.

Every time I talked with my best friends from high school during orientation we had a common refrain: "Does anybody remember how to make friends?" Although all of us had made various friends over our high school experiences (we weren't actually complete lepers), it had been a really long time since any of us, who all went to the same tiny school our entire lives, had to find completely new people.

And I think that's an important distinction: There's a difference between finding and making "friends" and finding your "people." Friends aren't too difficult to come by—they're on your hall, in your classes, other members of a club. It's easy enough to talk with them and enjoy spending time with them. But your "people" are your nonbiological family. They're the people you go to first with a problem and the ones you celebrate with when you meet someone special or get a great grade. Finding your people isn't always easy and is bound to take some time. Of course, there are always the stories of people who instantly connected with their freshman roommate the second they moved in, or found their friend soul mate during the first hall meeting. More likely than not, it's going

35

to take a little more scouring than that. But the key to remember is that you have to get through the somewhat false nonfriendships, the incessant shallow conversations, to allow the real ones to emerge. And emerge they will.

Annoyed. I can't be the only one who finds icebreakers, information sessions about how to best plan for your future academic experience, and mandatory viewings of fire safety videos to be *the worst*, can I? Although there may be some fun activities planned and good times to be had during orientation, there's always the necessary crappy part—the guidelines, the housekeeping, the administrative information. Basically, you just need to grin and bear it. Make a mental note to help run orientation later on so that you can make fun of the freshmen who will have to do the same thing when you're a smug, informed upperclassman—it makes the whole thing somewhat more tolerable.

Embarrassed. Chances are there will be some parties on campus during your orientation period. And I don't mean the organized activities the college has sanctioned for you that feel more like a middle school dance than an actual collegiate social experience, but the kind that involve prohibited libations. A word to the wise: A party during orientation is not the time to drink excessive amounts (especially if it's your first time drinking at all) or to generally exceed your limits in any big way. Stay alert and watch out for yourself and others. Although there may not necessarily be "reputations" on most college campuses the way there are in high school, orientation is still more like high school in that everybody is hyperaware of everybody else. Everyone feels super self-conscious and will gleefully grab any opportunity to point out other people's faux pas in the hopes of deflecting their own. Not to mention, this will be everybody's first impression of each other and first impressions are not only pretty important, but hard to make up for.

Although we'll talk about partying, alcohol, and drugs in depth later in this book, note that orientation is not the ideal time to start testing your limits; there will be plenty of time for that later on.

During orientation, just stay alert. Also, help out those who weren't given such advice. They'll (hopefully) thank you and remember that you were there for them, which could come in handy down the line—not to mention that it's just the right thing to do.

Luckily, orientation lasts for a finite period of time. Before you know it, school will be in full swing. Upperclassmen will swarm the campus, ready to get back into their routines. And although it can feel pretty overwhelming to still feel like you're desperately doggy paddling while everyone else is swimming with Michael Phelps-like speed and agility, it's all about perspective: Try not to view the transition into the true start of college as an attempt to melt into the stream, but as your first chance to truly emerge.

COLLEGE ISN'T A TIME OF "REINVENTION": IT'S ONE OF FREEDOM

There's a pretty pervasive myth that college is an opportunity for self-invention, that it's the best opportunity to reinvent yourself as the person you've always wanted to be. The idea is that shedding the skin of your high school self and designing a completely new one will allow you to be the best, happiest version of yourself—self-fulfillment *taken care of.*

But that presentation is seriously problematic. The idea that some manufactured version of yourself based on media cues, on what you think other "successful" women are like, will make you happy seems pretty false to me. There are undoubtedly countless ways to define happiness, and I'm sure those definitions have all been embroidered on an abundance of throw pillows around the world. But at its core, I'd argue that personal happiness is based on being well acquainted and comfortable with your *true* self—not some manufactured version of yourself cultivated from a variety of sources, including that perfect girl in high school that you'd totally hate if she weren't so damn lovable plus a Manic Pixie Dream Girl impression with a little bit of perfectly awkward Jennifer Lawrence candidness thrown in.

Impersonating the person you *think* you want to be won't make you happy because you'll constantly be performing, not living. It's only from the security produced by a strong sense of self that we can ever hope to even know *what* will make us happy, let alone how to go after it—not from inventing a totally new character to play. The problem is not that young women need to find a place where they can invent a totally new, seemingly better persona. It's that many of us *don't* authentically know who we are.

While finding one's identity isn't necessarily a gendered issue, it definitely impacts women in a uniquely intense way. In fact, 42% of college-aged women reported to one author that their foremost concern is self-identity (Rowe-Finkbeiner, 2004).

The tension between the pressure to project the identity of a "perfect" girl (size 0, straight-A, you know the drill) and to be ourselves is one in which many if not most young women are well versed. We are a generation of women bred to strive for perfection and consider anything less a personal failure. But while on paper we look like the women our grandmothers envisioned as they bore an unthinkable amount of crap for the outlandish goal of equality, in actuality many of us are stunted in a way that our résumés fail to capture. Although our academic vocabularies are robust, our emotional vocabularies are barren. Although we're incredibly driven and goal-oriented, we're completely disassociated from our authentic selves. We know who we're supposed to be, what we're supposed to look like (on paper and in person), but have no idea who we *actually* are, have no idea how to ask for what we *want*, have no idea what we even need.

Psychologist Roni Cohen-Sandler wrote about the relatively recent spike in stress among girls in 2006, writing that, "Girls . . .

are so focused on achieving external emblems of success that they don't get the chance to figure out what really excites them and gives them pleasure" (as cited in Simmons, 2009, p. 5). More recently, author and girl expert Rachel Simmons has identified this phenomenon as the "curse of the good girl." Simmons wrote in her 2009 groundbreaking book *The Curse of the Good Girl: Raising Authentic Girls With Courage and Confidence* that "Many of the most accomplished girls are disconnecting from the truest parts of themselves, sacrificing essential self-knowledge to the pressure of who they think they ought to be" (p. 5). So although we've never looked better on paper, we've (possibly) never *felt* weaker. The irony would be hilarious if it weren't so depressing.

Applying and going to college may very well be the first time young women, in a society that regularly objectifies and demeans us, are asked to invest in ourselves, to make a choice that will benefit us and revolves around our own self-fulfillment. But it's hard to make such a personal decision when we're bred to please others. We're raised to feel that we must eat, dress, and exist in a way that leads others to perceive us as beautiful. We're taught that our good grades aren't so much an indication of our personal knowledge and passion but of how "competitive" we are to attend a certain school. If we continue to attempt to be flawless ideals rather than authentic, flawed humans, how are we ever supposed to know what we *truly* want beyond what we're expected to want?

GET TO KNOW WHO YOU'VE ALWAYS BEEN

Despite the popular theory that college is *the* opportunity to invent a new persona for ourselves because of a more externally accepting environment, I'd argue that such an environment facilitates the first real opportunity to get to know who we've *always* been—but have been encouraged to repress. I think it's by becoming acquainted with that true self, by establishing an identity complete with self-confidence, self-esteem, and assertiveness, that we will feel secure and know where we will best fit and how we can make the most out of our college experience.

And luckily, college is *full* of opportunities to freely allow ourselves to figure out who we are. Here are just a few ways you can embrace this opportunity.

Try something you're afraid you'll be horrible at. Have you always loved singing, but only to the audience of your shampoo and showerhead? Have you always had strong opinions, but a fear of public speaking? Now is seriously one of your last chances to truly explore a hidden talent or unexplored interest. Any adult will tell you that once you're a "real person" with a "real job," it becomes infinitely more difficult to pursue such things. And who knows? You could get involved with something that changes your life—whether it changes the course of your study, shapes your social life, or just makes you feel fulfilled and happy, you wouldn't be the first person to be positively impacted by embracing the possibility of failure. Also, try to embrace fear whenever possible. If doing something terrifies you, it's one of the best reasons to pursue it. One of the things you'll likely find in college is that everything is at your fingertips if only you embrace fear and gather the courage to reach for it.

Speak your mind. My entire first semester of freshman year, I was too terrified to speak up in any of my classes. I was worried that my peers would judge what I was saying and think it wasn't insightful enough. I was hyperaware of my freshman status and assumed that upperclassmen had access to a wealth of knowledge that a lowly freshman like me couldn't comprehend, and therefore shouldn't challenge by speaking.

In retrospect, holding myself back from speaking was ridiculous. I was being hypercritical of myself: When I finally started speaking in my seminar classes, I never embarrassed myself, I just benefited from contributing to a discussion, which, it turns out, is a really valuable part of your education. I also realized there wasn't any blinking neon sign following me around, demarcating my freshman status—my comments and presence in class were taken at face value. A college education is not about sitting lifelessly in a lecture, alternating between taking notes, daydreaming about somehow being transported into an episode of *Scandal* as Olivia Pope's sidekick/BFF, and online shopping. It's about engaging. And I recognize that sounds like very official, textbook advice, but it's so true: You gain so much more by actively participating in your classes—it's the difference between being taught and *learning*. Also, being able to offer your opinion and speak in front of a group are *really* vital life skills—they'll be relevant and hugely important to whatever work you end up doing, I promise you that.

Befriend somebody you don't think you'll get along with. It's so easy to relegate yourself to hanging out with the same type of people you did in high school: If you're a theater person, it's easy to gravitate toward other people in the drama program; if you're an environmentalist, there are undoubtedly countless eco-enthusiasts ready to reach out to you. But college campuses are full of passionate students with unique talents and great intellect. Make it your personal mission to find somebody radically different from yourself and befriend him or her. Although it's great to find people who understand you on an intimate level, who can relate to you in a specific way, it's also vitally important to meet people who can expose you to completely different perspectives and values. Maybe the friendship will work in the long term and maybe it won't, but it will definitely be a valuable experience in some way.

Because you are a special snowflake, I can't tell you exactly what to do to establish your personal identity. But I will encourage you to try some of the aforementioned things so you can figure out who the hell you are. Our society does a good enough job of actively objectifying and sexualizing women and breeding us to believe that there is no deeper self to invest in beyond our bodies, which only exist to please and/or attract men, without us giving in and helping them. And what better venue to try to figure this out than one that's pretty forgiving and full of a bunch of diverse options and influencing forces, both academic and social?

BEING A MINORITY

But what if there are parts of your identity about which you are *very* sure and are proud of? How can you fully maintain these qualities, especially if they qualify you as a minority on your campus? For example, how can you hang on to your identity as a Black woman on a predominately White campus? How can you maintain your Jewish faith on a predominately Christian campus? Especially in the face of others' ignorance (which, unfortunately, still often persists even in supposedly "enlightened" academic spaces), how can you proudly express part of yourself that makes you somewhat different from the campus majority?

First and foremost, try to find an already established group of people who share your identity. Chapter 6 discusses cultural sororities, which offer ethnically and culturally specific social communities. Most campuses have LGBTQ-oriented clubs and/or a Gay-Straight Alliance Club as well as Hillel (a Jewish-based organization) and many other faith-based organizations. These various groups can be a great way to maintain your ethnic/religious/cultural identity within the context of a campus on which that identity qualifies you as a minority. If for some crazy reason a specific group that caters to your identity/values doesn't exist, start your own! If your college's admissions officers are at least baseline adequate at their jobs, you will not be the only person of your ethnic/religious/cultural group on campus, and therefore will likely be able to find others interested in joining forces with you.

But beyond finding a support system, it can be really difficult to deal with being a minority on an individual, everyday level—and there's no prescription for how to navigate that experience.

Out of the Mouths of ~~Babes~~ Current College Students

on Being a Minority

"I'm LGBTQ, and college has actually helped me deal with that. Christian high school was not the optimal setting to accept that, but I got involved with my university's GSA (Gay-Straight Alliance), and just knowing people who'd already been through this and interacting with them in person, rather than just online, helped me figure out how I wanted to make this a part of my life and integrate it into my self-expression. I'm active in the community of LGBTQ people at my university, and it all works because I've done it the way that feels most comfortable for me."

—Susan, Case Western Reserve University

"Being religiously observant on campus has been a great source of comfort for me, especially being so far from home. My involvement with Hillel, the Jewish Student Union on campus, has provided me with a network of friends and fellow community members who have similar values to me. I never feel like I am missing out when my other friends go out on Friday nights and I observe the Sabbath, because I know I'll be having my own fulfilling experience with people I care about and who understand and share that commitment."

—Leah, University of Pittsburgh

"My parents immigrated to the U.S. from Kenya. In college, I met a lot of first generation Americans with whom I could relate. Many of us were used to being the only minority in our classes and activities. I think I faced less discrimination in college than in Virginia, but I definitely felt uncomfortable at times. I think for minority students in particular, it's easy to feel like you don't belong. It's pretty likely that someone has made a remark to you along the lines of, 'you only got in because you are _____.' Those doubts on top of the doubt that everyone naturally has to deal with can be overwhelming. Try to find an adult—an advisor or professor that you can talk to, and seek out friends, from any background that value you and the experiences you bring to the table."

—Bunge, Barnard College

The first few weeks of (or even the entire first semester of) college can be legitimately scary. You'll probably struggle to figure out how you fit in—whether it's trying to find what makes you unique, or preserving what you know makes you different. But rather than letting these feelings overwhelm you, remember that college is ultimately a time of freedom. It can be difficult to let go of the person you've always tried to be, especially if you have no idea who you really are beneath that. It can be frustrating to try to fight to maintain aspects of your identity that set you apart. But persist, because becoming truly secure with your authentic self means setting yourself up for a life full of authentic self-fulfillment. It will lead to what *you* want, not what everybody has always told you to want. Don't let this opportunity pass you by.

CHAPTER 3

ACADEMICS

(oh, Right, College Is Also About Learning and Stuff)

An essential part of the college experience is certainly what you learn outside of the classroom (like deep universal truths about humanity and how to cook all of your meals using just a mug and a microwave—you know, the *truly* important stuff). But, believe it or not, what you learn in the classroom is also pretty valuable. So what *really* goes on in those classes?

When talking about college, we often take for granted the idea that school is school. It's acknowledged that college classes will inevitably be harder than high school classes but it seems to be assumed that succeeding in college academically is a matter of inherent intelligence, of pushing yourself harder if you're struggling. But, like literally every other aspect of college, I'm here to tell you that that's not quite the case—collegiate academics are not so cut and dry. But have no fear, there are definitely some tips and tricks that make academic success achievable for *everyone*, no matter what your grades were in high school and no matter how rough the transition to undergrad may feel at first.

promotion. Nobody is going to serve you helpful resources on a platter. Welcome to the world of adult accountability. There may be people available to help you achieve success, but it's ultimately your responsibility to motivate yourself to reach out to *them*, to encourage *yourself* to be the best possible version of yourself.

So, yes, college is more academically challenging than high school. But, as it turns out, incoming college freshmen usually don't struggle academically because they're not intelligent enough to handle the content of college classes. More often than not, it's the somewhat intangible challenges of college classes that trip up new students. But, luckily, there are plenty of ways to overcome the unique structural and organizational aspects of accomplishing collegiate work.

NOT TO FEAR!
SUCCESS IS POSSIBLE

HOW TO GET HELP

Now that I've painted a somewhat bleak picture of a life of complete independence, let me assure you that there are ways to deal with a new, challenging academic reality beyond sucking it up and realizing life is completely about self-reliance. Yes, you'll have to experiment, practice, and figure out what works best for you. But there are also various resources and individuals you can reach out to that will be willing to help you help yourself, including:

◇ WHOM to ask for help:

☞ *Your advisor:* Chances are, you'll be assigned an academic advisor (either randomly or based on an indicated major preference) at the beginning of your freshman year. Advisors are a great initial resource. Their job is to guide your quest to becoming an independent and functional student. They are there to give you advice on designing a schedule and to refer you to other resources at your school if you need help beyond their abilities.

- *A specific professor:* Chances are, you will develop an academic crush on one or more of your professors. Beyond physical attractiveness, this could also easily be spurred by their dreamy use of words like "epistemological" and "acculturation" without blinking and the way they cause your entire worldview to implode in an hour and a half or less. That's some straight up, weak-in-the-knees brain-sexiness. Don't be afraid to get to know such a particularly talented professor. Visit during office hours, ask probing questions about lectures, challenge the points he or she made—believe me, professors love it. Chances are if you take the time to let your professors know they're succeeding at inciting you to think, not only will your grade likely improve, but also you'll genuinely get a lot out of your conversation. It's these one-on-one conversations that may inspire a great paper topic or help you better understand the class material on a deeper level. Also—side note—many scholarships, study abroad programs, and

Out of the Mouths of ~~Babes~~ Current College Students

Academic Success

"Don't let people's bullshit convince you that everyone around you puts little to no effort into academics and then somehow miraculously gets all As and Bs. That's just not true. For some reason, in college it's *totally cool* to act like you don't try and still do well, but that's not really how it works. If you care about performing well in college, put in the effort. Literally the easiest thing you can do to get good grades in college is to just go to class. Making friends in class is also super helpful because you have someone to study with and oftentimes you'll encourage one another to do the work because you'll remind each other of upcoming assignments, due dates, etc."

—Nora, Barnard College

graduate school applications require a professor recommendation letter. On a more strategic level, you'll want to develop a good relationship with at least one or two professors so when the time comes, you can turn to them for a really great rec letter.

◊ **WHERE to get help:** One of the best kept secrets on most college campuses is the truly copious resources available to students—both academic in nature, as well as health-related (but we'll get to that in another chapter). Usually, colleges bury information about these resources in some giant information packet for incoming freshmen that literally nobody reads except for your mom (and whenever she tries to tell you about something she read in the packet you're like, "Shut up, Mom. I got this. I'm an adult now, OKAY?"). It turns out your campus may have/probably has:

☛ *A math and/or writing center:* These centers are often run by particularly gifted students at your college—usually upperclassmen—who are just *waiting* to help students develop a paper topic or demystify the way your math professor seems to be speaking English even though everything he or she says is completely incomprehensible. If you're struggling to write a paper or get through a problem set, these are *amazing* resources to have . . . and yet most students choose to struggle alone rather than to basically ensure a boosted grade and a better understanding of their academic material. Go figure.

☛ *A tutoring program:* Many colleges have tutoring programs that cater to areas more specific than the basic reading, writing, and arithmetic. I know my freshman year, many of my nonscientifically minded peers sought out tutors to help them through their various lab requirements. But tutoring isn't solely a freshman prerogative: I know upperclassmen who still seek out tutors for anything from economics to Spanish to computer science. Basically there's no shame in asking for help. There's no such thing as a subject that's "too easy" to seek help for, and you're never "too old" to need a helping hand. These resources exist for everybody for any reason—take advantage of them.

HOW TO STUDY

I've always thought it's weird that even starting in middle and high school, it's taken for granted that students just inherently know how to study in a way that's best suited to their particular learning style. The truth is, knowing how to study is an individualized skill that is hardly self-evident to most people. Figuring out how to study best is largely a process of trial and error—of trying different methods and seeing how you best process and remember information. But if you're at a complete loss, here are some general places to start:

◇ **WHOM to study with:** Studying in groups is a great way to process and remember information. Other students may raise questions or interesting points about the information that may not have occurred to you, they may be able to explain concepts in a way that resonates with you better than the way your professor did, and even explaining a concept to another student helps you better remember and understand it. Also, it's just a way to mix things up: Sitting alone with a book in your lap for hours on end is not only boring and depressing, but can be ineffective after a while. Your mind is bound to wander and at some point you're just wasting your time.

◇ **WHAT to study:** Between your reading, lecture notes, and discussion sections, you're going to end up with *way* more information available to study than you'll be tested on. Before you start studying in earnest, it can be helpful to go through all of these notes and highlight or write out separately key points or other things you *know* will be on the test so you're only focusing on the essentials. Knowing what information is essential often takes practice, though. It's a delicate, ever-changing balance of generally knowing what information you felt was key and what information your professor emphasized. There is no formula: Trust your intuition and dive in.

◊ **WHEN to study:** Cramming is definitely not the best way to study, and yet it's often the default option for super busy college students. Do yourself a favor and at least *attempt* to start studying for exams a week or at least a few days before D-Day. If you break up all of the material you need to cover over a few days, then it will inevitably seem more manageable and you'll be more likely to truly understand and remember it all. You'll also leave yourself time to e-mail professors and/or TAs or (better yet) visit their office hours and ask them questions in person. If you do go the cramming route, know your limits. And definitely give your mind some breaks—it's really not effective to study for hours on end. You're much more likely to benefit from studying for an hour and a half or so at a time with 15 minute breaks in between. Those breaks work as great incentives to get through your material. Also, showing up to a test after 8 hours of sleep and digesting a well-rounded breakfast is much more valuable then showing up to a test with 8 hours of studying and 47 cups of coffee under your belt.

◊ **WHERE to study:** Try to figure out early on in the semester where you work and concentrate the best. Some people have to be in a silent library, others prefer coffee shops with a low level of din, and others don't see the point in putting in the effort to look like a human (valid) and never leave their dorm rooms. Don't take for granted that wherever your friends are studying is the best place for you—experiment a little with different locations. You might be surprised to find that after weeks of following your friends to the library, you're actually much more comfortable in the student center, or you might discover that if you keep showing up to the same Starbucks, sometimes they'll throw you a free refill out of pity for your greasy, unwashed, and distressed state (which is *obviously* not something I know from experience).

◇ **WHY study:** There are, of course, college students who choose not to study at all. But here's the thing: On some level, you have to ask yourself what the hell you're doing at college if it's not ultimately to learn. There is, of course, a strong case to make for having fun (all work and no play and whatnot) but it would be a real shame to graduate from college and find that when given amazing academic resources and a real opportunity to enlighten and push yourself, you just slacked off and wasted your time. Basically, get it together and don't mess up this small window to open your mind in a really valuable way.

At the end of the day, academic success is a matter of trial and error, of practice, and of figuring out what works for you. There is a chance that your first semester of college may result in grades that would have given you a perfectionist-induced panic attack in high school: This is *normal* and even a common experience. Transitioning from high school to college is just that—a *transition*—and everybody takes her own time to adjust to new expectations and responsibilities. If you feel like you are making a genuine effort to learn how to prioritize and manage your work, that you're trying out strategies that work best for you in terms of the amount of time and effort you need to put into readings and assignments,

LIFE HACKS

The Beauty of Organization

Some people do not see the iridescent beauty that is a well-organized life. To those who do: Well, my Type A sisters, I salute you. To those who don't: Let me try to show you the light. Having a well-organized life will not only make everything easier, but may very well make your academic experience more efficient. Here are some organization tips:

♦ **Develop a filing system:** You're likely to have syllabi, handouts, and a ton of supplemental readings in addition to your textbooks or other assigned books for each class. Make sure you have a folder to file all of those papers (which you *always* end up needing to refer to or study again at some point) instead of letting them fall loosely away into the ether (the same place single socks and lip balms disappear into).

♦ **Use a planner/calendar:** This seems very Type-A and maybe it is, but actually documenting everything that you need to do makes accomplishing it all seem infinitely more manageable. Buy a planner, use the majestic miracle that is Google Calendar, develop an intricate sticky note system—no matter how you do it, itemize your life. Having everything laid out before you keeps all of your obligations relevant and keeps you from forgetting about each item altogether.

♦ **Embrace organizational technology:** I've heard that sometimes people use apps and technology to play games involving birds, words, and/or candy or send ugly selfies to their friends. That's nice, but I mostly use technology to organize my life. Some of my favorites include Google Drive (which allows you to create automatically updating, sharable documents, surveys, and beyond and is amazing for group work); When2Meet (http://when2meet.com—which visually represents when all members of a group are able to meet); Wunderlist (http://wunderlist.com—the ultimate to-do-list maker); and Mint (http://mint.com—which simplifies your financial life by syncing your checking, savings, and credit card accounts and breaks down your spending into a budget).

and that you are seeking help in the areas that challenge you most, then you're right on track, no matter what your transcript says.

The best way to succeed academically your first semester is to recognize and accept that you can't do everything perfectly—really, ever, but especially not at the very beginning of this new chapter of your life. You need to cut yourself some slack while at the same time avoiding the mindset that you're doomed to fail so why bother caring or trying. There's a way to not kill yourself trying to perfectly succeed while still putting in a solid and responsible effort—it's just up to you to figure out what that is.

THINKING AHEAD: PLANNING YOUR ACADEMIC CAREER

Talk to any college senior about her college experience and most are likely to say something like, "It just went by so fast." You might then catch a wistful sigh and a glimmer of a tear in her eye as she considers the horrible economy into which she is about to jump headfirst. But it's true: College does go by *so fast*. So although you should take freshman year as it comes and shouldn't enter college with a set idea of what you want to study or what you hope to accomplish in concrete terms, it's worth thinking ahead at least a little bit as you *will* need to make decisions—and the time to do so will arrive before you know it. From picking the first classes you'll take, to thinking about what major you might want to declare down the line, it's all worth considering (on a somewhat noncommittal basis) before you dive in headfirst.

CHOOSING YOUR CLASSES

Every school has a different approach to how incoming freshmen determine what classes they'll take. Some schools don't let students enroll until they arrive on campus. Others (like mine) send out information about classes—including classes specifically recommended for freshmen—over the summer and require that you select your classes at that point. Whatever the timing or method of class selection your school employs, here are some universal things to keep in mind as you select your courses:

◊ **Take it easy:** There will be plenty of time to challenge yourself in the coming years: Your first semester is not the time to try to get into several labs and senior seminars. It might be especially hard for those overachievers used to piling on the AP classes to take a step back, but remember: You're going to face a ton of new experiences and challenges in your first few months at school. You'll want to be able to devote a significant amount of time to all of these new experiences rather than be solely consumed by school. Don't slack off by any means, but be realistic about your course load (edging on the side of prudence).

◇ **Consider knocking out some general education requirements:** If you have no idea what classes to take first, getting those pesky requirements out of the way is a great place to start. At Barnard College, we have something called the "Nine Ways of Knowing" which, despite the deceptive nomenclature, is not in fact the title of a Greco-Roman philosopher's biologically ignorant philosophy of human nature but rather a set of requirements Barnard students must complete before graduating. Many Barnard students majoring in the humanities try to end the evil hold the numbers have over their lives by knocking out the math and science related requirements right away, whereas the premed kids tackle classes in the domains of literature or "Cultures in Comparison" so they can focus on figuring out how to save other humans' lives and stuff.

◇ **Try to get into the class of a beloved professor:** There are plenty of sites out there that rate professors (like http://ratemyprofessors.com as well as plenty of university specific sites). If you don't know what subject you might be interested in, signing up for a class with a really great, inspiring professor is as good a place as any to start. In fact, it's common knowledge among most college students that (generally) a professor is a much better indicator of whether or not you'll enjoy a class than the subject matter: A great professor can make anything interesting, whereas a horrible professor can make an interesting topic intolerable.

◇ **Think ahead toward your major:** I am in no way advocating for declaring your major your freshman year. In fact, you should absolutely keep an open mind—and therefore explore classes in multiple areas that pique your interest so you can get a taste of everything that's out there before you make any decisions. However, if you are considering a pre-professional track, sometimes in order to graduate on time you'll have to start pretty much right away. In that case, you'll want to sign up for your labs and whatnot immediately so you don't fall behind in an already rigorous academic course. And speaking of thinking about your major . . .

Out of the Mouths of ~~Babes~~ Current College Students

Making Academic Choices

"One thing that annoyed me freshman year is the dissonance between the rhetoric that you have all this time to explore and the reality that you have to make choices. Your freshman year is an enormous blank slate and there are a lot of things you could pursue but for a lot of majors, unless you know what you want to do your freshman fall you're then left playing catch up. There were so many people who said their freshman fall that they were pursuing computer science and I was just like 'How do you know what that is?' That was in no way something I had any exposure to as a city public school kid and I felt if I wanted to pursue it I would have to play catch up. The truth is you do have to close some doors in order to pursue certain things."

—Miranda, Stanford University

CHOOSING YOUR MAJOR

In my experience, incoming freshmen usually approach their major in one of two ways: Either they self-consciously have absolutely no idea what they want to do or they are dead set on pursuing a very specific path. There are few students who may have a vague interest in a few areas or who have faith that by jumping into college they will find the path that's right for them (or at least there are few who are willing to admit it). But, as it turns out, that might just be the best approach of all.

About half of college students will change their majors even after declaring (Capuzzi Simon, 2012). Perhaps that's because many schools offer an incredible variety of majors (for instance, the University of Michigan offers 251 majors) and majors in fields that incoming freshmen couldn't even imagine before taking a class in that domain (Capuzzi Simon, 2012). How would you know that you have a passion for puppetry before taking puppeteering classes at the University of Connecticut or that you can actualize your dreams of becoming a survivalist through Plymouth State University's Adventure Education major? (Ehley, 2013).

Most schools won't require you to actually declare your major until the second semester of your sophomore year (and you probably shouldn't before then), but here are some tips for getting an early start on thinking about your major.

Take general ed classes or classes that seem interesting first. If I hadn't decided to take the class "Social Movements" in order to fill my "Social Analysis" general education requirement, I probably never would've declared sociology as my major. I was actually dead set on majoring in women's studies (despite the *endless* jokes of "But why isn't there a men's studies?" in response to my choice—to which I'd respond "That's called history," but I digress). Then I took "Social Movements" and realized I was much better suited for sociology. But even if you don't have requirements to fill, don't be afraid to take a class in a discipline that seems a little offbeat or uncharacteristic. You just never know if you'll happen upon an area of study you're surprisingly passionate about.

But beyond possibly encountering a new, awesome discipline, filling your general requirements just buys you some time to give your major some more thought. It allows you to get to know yourself better in other capacities—development that could easily lead to a better understanding of what you need and want to get out of your education.

Be honest with yourself. There's nothing wrong with knowing what you want and going after it. If you're sure you're destined to be a doctor, a philosopher, or a linguist, then go for it. But make sure to periodically check in with yourself and confirm that you are enjoying what you're doing and the classes you're taking. It's important to pursue a path not because you think you should or because you always told yourself you would, but because you're actually happy doing it and are getting something out of it. Especially if you're preprofessional (and especially if your parents pushed that track on you), just keep tabs on the way you feel about your course of study. You should enjoy and feel inspired by your education, not feel obligated to pursue a certain course.

And just remember . . . The dirty secret about most majors—and most of a liberal arts education in general, for that matter—is that *very few* majors DIRECTLY translate to what you end up doing with your life. For example, consulting and finance firms actually frequently recruit humanities majors *because* of their more creative approach to problem solving. Most anthropology majors probably don't end up actually doing extensive ethnographies for the rest of their lives, and many psychology majors hardly end up listening to and analyzing other people's problems (or at least they do on their own time in a thing called friendship). That's why it's so important to *enjoy* your major—for most intensive purposes, it's just a more structured way to enjoy the learning process and explore themes and concepts that fascinate you than it is professional training.

Also, keep an eye out for possible minors. A lot of students accidentally complete minors after taking multiple classes in an area of interest. If you feel like you're taking a lot of classes in an area technically outside of your major, check and see what that department's minor requirements are—you may have already completed them (or only need to take another class or two to do so . . . and at that point, why not?).

THE BOTTOM LINE: HOW TO BALANCE WORK AND LIFE

There are countless "self help" books out there that claim to give you the key to happiness, the *secret to life*. These books pose some interesting theories about visualizing the reality you want, about changing yourself to create the ideal life—the suggestions go on and on. But if you ask me, there is no singular prescription for finding happiness. Happiness can only be found in a balanced life, and balance depends on the unique struggles and goals of each individual. I mean, yes, this is coming from a 20-year-old whose only solid life goals are to (in the short term) eat a cupcake and to (in the long-term) round out the magical Tina Fey-Amy Poehler friendship into a trio. But hear me out.

Life is about balance for everybody, but it has a specific socio-cultural meaning for women. Women are expected to flawlessly balance work and life; it's an impossible juggling act that college women (until arguably very recently) were not even aware they would face. We largely took for granted that we could have careers *and* families—we assumed that everything would fall into place. We certainly feel the strain of balancing our lives while we're in school: We struggle to accommodate club meetings, rehearsals, and jobs with imminently due papers, seeing friends, and maybe going on a date or two (haha), hopefully finding a couple of hours to sleep somewhere in there. But what we don't realize is that once we graduate, once we enter the "real" world rather than the insulated quasiworld of our college campuses and try to have careers instead of jobs and "serious" relationships instead of hook ups, we are faced with ratcheted up, competing demands.

I think our generation seriously needs to amend this picture of our future, largely by refusing to settle for anything less than equal partnerships in which our partners put exactly the same amount of work into our home lives as we do and by relieving ourselves from the perfectionist standards that incite us to try to achieve EVERYTHING in the first place. But, until then, I think actively practicing healthy ways of balancing our lives in college can do a lot to make the future balancing act that may dominate our adult lives a little more manageable. If we establish habits and routines that allow us to balance work (school) with our lives (friendships, relationships, and fun) we just might be able to carry them with us throughout our lives.

So how do we do this? I honestly have a problem with various lifestyle blogs and lady-specific magazines that claim to solve all of your problems with self-evident advice like "just breathe" (I'm pretty sure I do), "slow down!" (unrealistic), or "meditate" (I would if I had even a modicum of patience). So here are some platitude-free things college women can and should do to actually force some balance into their lives.

Schedule time devoted to your weakness. Maybe this is just the confluence of my Type A personality and visual learning style, but I find it incredibly helpful to take some time to plan out my week. Yes, this takes time and yes, nearly all of the events are subject to change (largely due to everybody else's insane schedules and the general flakiness of college students) but I find having everything laid out before me somehow makes everything seem much more manageable: My life is not just a swirling mass of commitments polluting my mind, popping up every time I'm just about to fall asleep—it's all there, ready to be checked off.

But beyond laying out everything I need to do and when I need to do it, I find it's helpful to schedule in time to attend to your weakness—to schedule balance into your life. If you're an incredibly social person, schedule in time where you absolutely have to work. If you're incredibly driven and prone to getting caught up in school, schedule in time where you have to take it easy and give your brain a break (hi mindless chick-flick marathon) or (better yet) when you allow yourself to go out and be social.

CHAPTER 4

MIND, BODY, AND SPIRIT

How to Keep (All Parts of) Yourself Alive and Well

So here's a fun fact about being a real, live, autonomous human being: You are the only person in charge of keeping yourself alive. This sounds pretty basic. You've been alive for, what, around 18 years? Sure, your parents helped out with the whole avoiding mortality thing (especially those first few years)—we have to give credit where credit is due. But, come on, do we really need to talk about keeping ourselves healthy?

Yeah, we really do. As it turns out, when faced with the complete inundation of new experiences and stresses that are part and parcel of your freshman year, it's the most basic stuff—like your health and well-being—that tend to go out the window first in an effort to stay afloat. And that's a serious problem, because if you don't feel well—in mind, body, and/or spirit—then you'll never be able to fully appreciate or perform well any other part of your college experience.

Also, you'll face many *new* facets of well-being. From new eating (and drinking) habits to various new ways of experiencing and taking care of your body, to tending to an overworked, constantly challenged mind, you're going to have a lot thrown at you. It turns out that really, truly taking care of yourself involves quite a bit more than flossing and begrudgingly eating your vegetables. Welcome to the adult world of health and wellness.

PHYSICAL HEALTH

When we hear the word *health*, we tend to mentally zip to images of body builders with disturbingly bulging veins and stores devoted solely to selling organic artisanal vegetable juices that taste intolerable yet promise to make you a human Thor. Or at least that's what my mind goes to. It seems like if you're following media cues, our options are that version of uber-health or succumbing to the obesity epidemic. But being healthy doesn't have to be this polarized: There is definitely a happy medium we can (and should) strive for.

Beyond striking a balance, it's important to remember that physical health should be about how you feel, not about how you look. This is often difficult for women to fully realize at any point in our lives (thanks Photoshop), but often becomes a serious point of contention in college, when our defenses are down due to the many other sources of stress, confusion, and the process of identity formation many of us go through. And it often strikes us in a few very specific ways.

THE MYTH OF THE FRESHMAN 15

There are a lot of crazy, scare-mongering myths floating around about the Freshman 15, but there is just one thing you need to know about it. Are you ready for this pearl of wisdom? Is your pen poised on paper, ready to capture my infinite knowledge? Okay, here it is: The Freshman 15 is COMPLETE AND UTTER BULLSHIT.

I'll level with you: There is truth to the idea that your body may very well change your freshman year. In fact, a 2011 study revealed that while the average female does gain about 3.1 pounds her freshman year, 25% of freshman actually *lose* weight and plenty won't notice a change in their weight at all (Zagorsky & Smith, 2011). It's also worth noting that this weight gain likely has less to do with being in college than it does with being an 18(ish)-year-old woman who is still developing. In fact, the average freshman gains less weight than does someone the same age who doesn't go to college (Zagorsky & Smith, 2011). So how many people actually do gain 15 pounds or more? Just under 10% of college freshmen according to the aforementioned study (Zagorsky & Smith, 2011). So yeah, consider the myth of the Freshman 15 BUSTED.

But the whole "Freshman 15" thing is ridiculous even *beyond* its basic factual inaccuracy. It's pretty unhealthy to compare your body to any kind of overarching norm or expectation. Instead, accept that you are still young and at a physiological stage where your body can (and probably will) still change. Instead of freaking out about weight gain or weight loss, focus on maintaining a weight and, more importantly than a specific number, a general feeling about your body that's right for *you.*

That being said, the reality is that freshman year is a time of serious life changes—and that undoubtedly extends to your eating and exercising habits. So although my life view can generally be summed up as: "Screw impossible beauty standards, love your body, and enjoy your life," there are also some nutrition-related changes you should be aware of from a perspective of health and practicality.

Beware of dining hall food. Despite many dining halls' attempts to offer vegan/gluten-free/low-fat/even-more-inedible-than-usual choices, most food exchanged for a meal card swipe is notoriously high in fat and calories and low on nutrition. We may be warned about this in terms of weight gain (as it turns out, nutritionists don't advocate eating fries and brownies for every meal for a reason), but it's also important to consider the nutritional content of food you consume in terms of your overall health. For instance, I chalked up feeling tired *all of the time* my freshman year to my increased workload and happily sustained an impressive dedication to an all carb diet. It wasn't until I was home for Winter Break and my mom made it her short-term life mission to constantly shovel vegetables into me like gas into a Hummer that I realized, *Oh, there's a REAL REASON why we should eat nutritious food—it HELPS US FUNCTION!* Which sounds ridiculously self-evident, but it's worth remembering, especially in the context of a culture that almost exclusively talks about food in terms of weight loss rather than health. It turns out eating well is not just about how you look, but very much (and more importantly) about how you feel and how well you function.

A changed activity level. The thing about (ostensibly) studying a lot and going to class is that you will not be required to move too much. This may seem great to my sisters in the cult of laziness (the introduction of the Snuggie was like a religious epiphany for me), but it's also pretty dangerous. Although moving might not be our definition of a good time, it's still necessary to at least attempt sometimes. Again, although we often talk about exercising in terms of weight loss (ugh, make it stop), it turns out exercise is actually really great for your physical as well as mental health.

Now I'm no doctor, but from what I understand, humans are physical beings: We were designed to move. Therefore, it's probably good to actually give our muscles something to do every once in a while. But beyond the benefits of ultra-low-grade body-building, you'd be amazed by how powerful endorphins are. There is nothing quite like the postexercise high, especially if you're feeling really worn down from studying and stress. It's counterintuitive, but usually when you feel really burnt out from studying, going to the gym and running for even just 20 or 25 minutes can give you an empowering boost of energy.

Bottom line: I can pretty much guarantee your campus has some form of a gym. Make an effort to get there on some kind of regular basis, or, better yet, sign up for some kind of exercise class that provides structure and external motivation to move your butt! Your Snuggie will be there for you when you get back, I promise.

Newly available (calorie-packed) alcoholic beverages. Of course, college freshmen don't drink *ever* because *it's illegal*. But it's probably worth noting on a GENERAL LEVEL that a surprising number of freshmen don't seem to realize that alcoholic beverages have calories—*a ton* of them, in fact. An average serving of beer contains 153 calories, and a serving of vodka or tequila has 97 (National Institute on Alcohol Abuse and Alcoholism, n.d.). That might not sound too bad, but few people successfully limit themselves to just one drink in a party setting and many consume multiple drinks multiple times a week. That's a lot of excess calories (math is fun). So if you're exercising and eating well and still feel like you're gaining weight, you may not be factoring in those (totally hypothetical) alcoholic beverages. It's important to remember: Everything is best *in moderation*. The same goes for other indulgences, like sweets or snacks. There's nothing inherently evil about them—in fact, they're pretty fantastic if I do say so myself. But if you've come to memorize the exact contents of your dorm's vending machine and are visiting it on an hourly basis, you may want to reevaluate your life choices.

Food = Comfort. I've said it before and I'll say it again: The transition to college is really difficult for many women. Food can seem like an obvious way to gain some comfort in an otherwise uncomfortable situation. Plenty of young women navigate the dining hall from an emotional perspective rather than from one of hunger or health. Any other guidebook might try to slap you on the wrist and say "DON'T EAT EMOTIONALLY. YOU'LL GET FAT" and leave it at that. Not me—let me just say I *completely* get that impulse. For a long time, I ate my feelings, too. But the thing about emotional eating beyond "making you fat" is that it's just not an effective way to deal with your feelings. It's a vicious cycle: You'll keep eating, but you'll never truly feel better because you're not dealing with the root of your feelings, you're just trying to smother them. Focus on actively thinking about moderate portions of food and incorporate fruits and veggies into every meal (they should take up about half of your plate, according to experts). If you still feel lost in a sea of buffet-style choices, try to remember how you ate at home (when food wasn't unlimited). If you actively make moderate decisions about your food instead of letting your heart guide your plate, you'll likely design a better meal for yourself.

Basically, I'm really annoyed and frankly bored with the ridiculous and repetitive "conversation" about women and the Freshman 15 (and eating and dieting in general, for that matter). We're constantly bombarded with strategies about how to eat to produce the "best" (i.e., thinnest) bodies. I say screw that—which, of course, is easier said than done, especially your freshman year. But here are some keys to remember about eating and nutrition:

◇ **Be gentle with yourself:** Don't psyche yourself out about the Freshman 15 . . . but don't down 20 shots a weekend followed by an entire pizza, either. Accept that you may very well gain weight—and if you do, the world as you know it won't implode. Focus on eating in a way that makes you feel healthy and whole, beyond any kind of number on a scale or nutrition label.

◇ **Remember changes in your body may be out of your control:** From a biological perspective, college-aged women commonly gain weight. In fact, women between the ages of 18 and 30 gain an average of 2.2 pounds per year ("Help, I Am Gaining Weight in My 20s!," 2010). It's a time of development and your body may change beyond a response to your new environment and life. This is called nature, and though media images try to encourage dieting away that extra layer of fat women naturally have for things like, oh, I don't know, CHILD BIRTH, it's really okay and even natural for us to have a body shape described by euphemisms like "curvy" or "full" (and which I call "powerful").

◊ **Everything in moderation:** It's really okay to enjoy your life, and that can often mean indulging in things that aren't necessarily "healthy" for you. Have that late night piece of pizza with your friends. Have cake on your roommate's birthday. As long as you don't eat less-than-healthy food for every meal, every single day in obscenely huge amounts, you'll be fine.

WHEN OUR BODY BECOMES THE ENEMY: NEGATIVE BODY IMAGE AND EATING DISORDERS

Although we accept that we'll be challenged intellectually and will face a new, adult reality in college, we are often unprepared for the way our bodies are included in our new intellectual and emotional struggles: Our bodies are often the sites for this struggle and the receptacle of our frustration and exploration.

Our generation has undeniably been inundated with and has internalized negative images and conceptions of unrealistic standards of beauty practically since birth in an unprecedented way. This struggle hardly abates in college. Eating disorders, as well as a general disordered body image, run rampant among college-aged women. In fact, 95% of those who have eating disorders are between the ages of 12 and 25.8 (National Association of Anorexia Nervosa and Associated Disorders [ANAD], 2013). According to ANAD (2013), 91% of women surveyed on a college campus had attempted to control their weight through dieting, while 22% diet "often" or "always." And despite the fact that eating disorders are often stereotyped as an affluent White girl problem, studies show that women of color are as likely to binge and purge, and are actually more likely to fast and abuse laxatives or diuretics. No matter our background, college-age women are all equally susceptible to falling into these traps (Brodey, 2005).

But what is it about college specifically that can so strongly impact the way we view and treat our bodies?

Perfect girls, perfect students, perfect bodies. Female college students tend to be pretty competitive. They're used to constant pressure to be the best, to achieve as much as possible to get into the school of their dreams—a pressure that permeates their entire existence. As Courtney Martin (2007) notes in *Perfect Girls, Starving Daughters,*

> Unfortunately, the insistence on perfection bleeds straight from the brain into the body: from perfect test scores and grades to perfect fitness and physique . . . Researchers and psychologists confirm that girls most likely to develop an eating disorder, or plain old obsession with fitness and food, are high achievers: many attend the best colleges in the nation. (p. 213)

One might think that getting into college would ease that burden, and might reduce the need for a stress coping mechanism like binging or purging. But in fact, as a 2004 Canadian study found, "education appears to be more important than occupationally defined social class in explaining body dissatisfaction" (McLaren & Kuh, 2004, p. 1583). Perfectionism is not a switch that can be turned off—especially for bright women, constantly pushing themselves to be "better."

It almost seems counterintuitive: Shouldn't intelligent women know better than to starve themselves, than to abuse their bodies? Don't they arguably have better access to information that indicates that these practices are wildly unhealthy and destructive? Actually, most do, but that hardly matters. British psychologists Helga Dittmar and Sarah Howard (2004) describe the phenomenon of young women who generally oppose an unattainable standard of beauty yet personally fall prey to those very ideas as a marked contrast between awareness of ideals versus internalization. These women silently suffer from a double dose of guilt: They feel guilty for fighting for society to redefine its standards of beauty while never feeling good enough themselves due to internalizing those same messages and despite "knowing better." It's a serious Catch-22.

Eating disorders aren't always about food . . . or even your body. It's well documented that eating disorders aren't *just* a response to feeling "fat"—they can function as coping mechanisms, especially in times of vulnerability and fear, two emotions that are in full supply when making the transition to college (Segal & Smith, 2013). Some young women view an eating disorder as a way to instill control in a world that seems to have completely shifted overnight: They feel that the only way to cope with an external environment seemingly beyond their control, with changing support networks and different routines, is to turn inward, to impose sanctions on their own body and derive power from the concrete effects they produce. In reality, they just lose more control as their *disorder* starts to dictate their feelings and actions.

But what can I actually DO? There are few sources of real, concrete advice for how to productively combat an eating disorder or negative body image. There's a valid reason for that: There are very few concrete things to be done in the face of a variety of intersecting unfortunate social realities based on myriad causes including centuries of ingrained sexism that ultimately cause these feelings and behaviors among women. The ultimate goal may be to put an end to the destructive society that is at the core of these feelings eventually, but, pragmatically, that may take a little while yet. In the meantime, here are a few productive tips to keep in mind that will hopefully help you or a friend consider this grossly sexist reality in a way that's much healthier and productive for you.

◊ If you feel you have negative body image:

☞ *Realize that this is bigger than you.* Most young women who feel dissatisfied with their bodies tend to feel that it is an individual experience. Most of us understand that negative body image is a struggle for many women, but that understanding is more cerebral than it is something that productively allows us to manage and moderate our feelings. But here's the thing—being able to really deconstruct the way negative body image is deeply embedded in society and enforced by external sources does *so* much to moderate those feelings. Understanding that billion dollar beauty industries make a ton of money by making us feel badly about our bodies (so that they can then sell us crap to "fix" them), that we have lived in the context of a society that sought to limit and oppress women in any way possible, including encouraging us to feel held back by our bodies, for centuries does so much to make this struggle feel less like a personal failure and more like an external roadblock.

☞ *Fake it until you make it.* Externalizing the insecurities trapped in our heads can make them feel more tangible and manageable. If you actively practice externalizing self-acceptance and self-love, soon enough it won't feel as forced. Self-love is at the root of any good relationship (with yourself, of course, but with others as well) and at the root of success. Actively practicing self-love is necessary to eventually achieving it, so regularly tell yourself you're beautiful (seriously). Also, focus on making mindful choices that are right for *you*. Remember, you have no idea what's going on in others' heads (but chances are it's a terrifying web of their own insecurities): You can only know what you think and what you need, so practice silencing the other voices and simply, clearly asking yourself what your needs are, then do your best to fulfill them.

- *Just say screw it.* This is way easier said than done, but good lord, hating yourself is *exhausting*. Like beyond being stupid and completely self-destructive and unhealthy, it actually just takes up SO MUCH TIME. It takes up so much space in your mind, so much emotional energy—energy you could expend on something that actually matters. You can't be digitally altered to perfection like models in advertisements. You are not a frat boy's ideal (nor would you ever want to be that pornified, two-dimensional version of a human). The sooner you accept and embrace the irrefutable reality of your individuality, the sooner you'll start really enjoying your life. Because here's the secret the beauty/weight loss/plastic surgery industries don't want you to know: Physically changing whatever you're insecure about won't make you happy. The process of trying to change yourself will make you miserable and you'll soon realize that life's difficulties still happen to conventionally attractive people. Focus on living *your* life.

◊ **If you feel you have an eating disorder:** I am by no means an expert on eating disorders or how to treat them. Luckily, though, there are plenty of resources out there, such as:

- *The National Eating Disorders Association* (NEDA; http://www.nationaleatingdisorders.org): NEDA campaigns for eating disorder prevention, has made treatment more accessible, and has increased funding related to eating disorder research. It also has a helpline that can offer some immediate support and guidance (1-800-931-2237) as well as a chat helpline available through its website.

☞ *Overeaters Anonymous* (OA; http://www.oa.org): OA uses a 12-step program to help individuals recover from compulsive eating by addressing underlying physical, emotional, and spiritual issues.

☞ *Your campus's health center*: Chances are, your campus's health center also has eating disorder related resources, such as a peer-support group or medical professionals knowledgeable about the topic and able to direct you to the help you need.

What if OTHER people have eating disorders or make you feel badly about the way you look? Did you ever have a moment (or many) in a high school cafeteria when a friend ("friend") looked at something delicious on your plate and passive aggressively said something like, "Wow, I wish I could eat like that," or "Are you sure you really want to eat that?" You're probably more than eager to leave behind those messed up frenemy relationships in high school.

Except, the thing is, these girls don't just disappear in college, and they're not always immediately identifiable. If you become really close with a girl like this, you might end up eating with her frequently, which means regularly surrounding yourself with this destructive mentality. So what do you do if you (otherwise) like this girl, but feel uncomfortable with these comments and especially if you start to feel like they're getting to you on a deeper level?

◇ **Be transparent:** In some ways, this is the most obvious thing to do but also the hardest. Be open and honest about your own struggles. Try to talk about how you worry about your body image (we all do to some extent)—and especially how you work through it. Never underestimate how being transparent about *anything* you struggle with can be the best way to help others who may have felt like they were the *only* one struggling with the same thing. Feeling less alone, like a problem isn't reflective of a personal failing, can be indescribably therapeutic and productive. Nip weird comments about food in the bud: Be upfront and tell your friend you feel those types of comments and mentality are destructive.

◇ **Remember, it's not about you:** Girls who make shaming comments about the way you eat don't think you're fat—they think *they're* fat. Beyond any reality about her body or your body, girls who make these comments are ultimately deeply affected by a society that encourages women to feel insecure about themselves. Though it might seem like she's being aggressive, she's actually crying out for help. Once you realize that feeling personally offended by her comments is futile, it'll take you to a mental space where you may meet her comments with compassion, which is what she really needs.

I personally know what this struggle can feel like. My freshman year, in an effort to appear as if I was thriving when I actually felt lost and helpless, I took my feelings of confusion and desperation out on my body—playing into the very stereotypes and standards this sexist culture asked me to.

Although I had struggled with body image in high school, I always thought that somehow I would just outgrow it and any other personal struggles in college: I figured I would be with peers who understood me, in an environment that suited my values and therefore (I implicitly reasoned), I would naturally feel better about myself on *all* levels. However, I didn't deal with the transition to college well, and my body took the biggest brunt of that difficult adjustment.

I allowed my body to become what I felt like was my only constructive project, the only thing I felt like I was making progress toward and the only thing that felt controllable in a life of new chaos. Everybody around me, influenced by a society that equates weight loss with self-improvement, viewed my weight loss as a success, as an indication that I was doing well and taking on my new life with gusto rather than an indicator that I was deeply struggling.

Over Winter Break, though, I realized that something needed to change: Something beyond hoping I would magically age out of

Your Other Syllabus

Important Body Image Reading Material

Like I said, understanding the way in which negative body image is a societal epidemic rather than just a personal issue is a really critical step toward learning how to love your body and reach some sense of peace about it. Seriously, reading these books and blogs changed my life: They helped me realize it was possible to actually love my body. They might not be the kind of *Sisterhood of the Traveling Pants/Gossip Girl/Twilight* books that you whip out for a mindless beach read, but TRUST ME, they will blow your mind.

Books

Perfect Girls, Starving Daughters by Courtney Martin: This book astutely captures how obsessions with food and weight hold young women back—and how we can all redirect the energy we spend denying ourselves contentment toward becoming the successful women we are all capable of being.

The Beauty Myth by Naomi Woolf: Woolf examines how the pressure for women to be beautiful has increased largely as a form of backlash to our increasing power. In this way, Woolf argues, the pressure to be beautiful isn't personal, but a social, economic, and political tool.

Fat Is a Feminist Issue by Susie Orbach: In this groundbreaking book, Orbach makes the case for fat-acceptance—for an individual's right to be happy and healthy at any size.

Blogs

Adios Barbie (http://adiosbarbie.com): This fantastic blog promotes a healthy body image and identity for people of all sizes, races, ages, sexual orientations, and abilities. Basically, it will make you feel awesome about yourself.

About-Face (http://www.about-face.org): About-Face is a nonprofit organization that provides tools and knowledge for women to understand and resist harmful media messages that affect their self-esteem and body image.

The Representation Project (http://www.missrepresentation.org/blog): This blog—an off-shoot of the documentary *Miss Representation* (a MUST SEE if you get the chance)—calls out the ways in which the media promotes negative body image and objectifies women.

the way I always inscribed my personal feelings on my body and, beyond that, the way this society defines women by their bodies and encourages them to do just that.

As it turned out, being kind to my body—the culturally indicated receptacle of blame for all of these feelings of internalized sexism—is work. I realized that in order to transgress something so universal, I had to stop categorizing myself: not as a straight-A student or as the person having the most fun ever at college. Radically, I had to think of myself as an individual and my body as my own, free from the normalized oppression of perfectionism and shaming of our bodies and our selves as women which impacts us on individual levels, but also impedes women's achievement overall. Especially in college, women are so distracted by our bodies, by the shame and blame we feel on a daily basis, that we're less productive and feel less capable of advocating for ourselves. The very things we go to college to achieve—career success, ambitions, and leadership potential—are hampered due to the way we equate insecurities about our bodies with our sense of worth on all levels. We don't view ourselves as the subjects of our own lives, but rather as objects, and women's progress overall is suffering because of it. Although it's difficult, the change has to start now, in college, when we still have a shot at reclaiming our bodies and refusing to let them hold us back from achieving all that we're capable of.

EMOTIONAL HEALTH

If you know anything about college, it's probably that it's supposed to be the best 4 years of your life. The truth is (as I've hopefully made abundantly clear by now), college is a *really* big transition—one that isn't quite the carefree experience everybody makes it out to be. In fact, framing it that way produces a *lot* of social and psychological pressure that can often—somewhat counterintuitively—produce a lot of new emotions that are challenging to navigate. And, unfortunately, nobody is really honest enough about this before you're thrown into it. There are plenty of things that may trigger emotional challenges, including these specific triggers:

◇ **Stress:** This may be the most obvious mental strain on college students, but alas, it is the most universal and consistent. Students of *all* ages bump up against stress on a pretty much continuous basis and, sadly, it seems that few ever really develop an effective strategy for dealing with it. Many (if not most) just accept it as a permanent aspect of life and let it slowly erode their well-being. Super healthy.

☛ *Solution:* Although you probably can't eliminate stress from your life, you can put effort into developing certain skills that can make a world of difference in terms of how you interact with it. Time management is essential: Try scheduling out everything you have to do so it feels more manageable. Force yourself to carve out time devoted to self-care—to doing something just for *you*. Get to know your own work patterns and don't give into the social construct of stress culture (what others do or *claim* to do to get their work done) and focus on what *you* need to do to get what *your* work done. Also refer to Chapter 3 on academics for more tips on how to manage stress and balance your life.

◇ **Social pressure:** So many rising freshmen are under the impression that they'll show up at school and good time on good time will fall into their lap. The truth is (as we will discuss further in Chapter 6), there's an art to having a healthy and well-rounded social life in college, and yet there remains this overarching ideal of college socializing that generates a weird pressure to have a ton of friends, to party all of the time, and more and more to *document* that fun. Social media has a uniquely deleterious effect on *everybody's* social life (no matter what they say). Everybody at some point or another has gone on Facebook and felt like everybody else was having *so much* more fun than them based on their photos and status updates. FOMO (Fear Of Missing Out, for the older family members reading this book) is a real thing for our generation: We're constantly convinced that there's something great going on somewhere without us, which is stressful in its own way.

☛ *Solution:* Remember that this social pressure REALLY IS universal, no matter how anybody else comes off or how social she claims to be. Nobody can have a super awesome fantastic time always, and everybody falls claim to FOMO at some point or another. Just try to focus on doing things that *you* think are fun and surrounding yourself with people who share those interests. Seriously, if partying isn't your thing, you're not going to have a good time with a group that wants to go clubbing every week. On some level, you have to ask yourself *why* you feel like you need to go along with social conventions that don't interest you or aren't fun for you. Also, don't be afraid to say no. There is no reason to try to be everywhere at once and at some point it'll stop being fun and will just seem like another series of obligatory commitments. Life (and the college experience itself) is way too short to engage in things you think you're *supposed* to. Do what you *want* to do and screw the rest. You'll be a lot happier for it.

◇ **Constant change:** One aspect of college that I was barely aware of before I was thrown into the thick of things is the fact that you have to deal with change *constantly*. It comes in all forms: from the more concrete—the fact that classes change every semester, that you'll likely switch where you live every year—to the intangible—a high turnover in hook ups, relationships, and even friendships. It's really easy to feel like the ground beneath your feet is anything but solid. Everybody around you is trying to figure out who they are, emotionally, intellectually, etc. and so are you. It's a process that necessitates adjustment and experimentation, which can mean that people and certain experiences may virtually disappear from your life relatively soon after they enter it. It's actually *a lot* to manage, especially if you're somebody who doesn't deal well with change anyway.

☛ *Solution:* This one's a little more difficult to get a handle on. Change is just difficult and, especially in terms of friendships and relationships, can lead to some messy emotions and heartbreak. The most salient tip I can possibly give is to first try to develop a really solid relationship with yourself. If you work intently on figuring out and knowing on a deeper level who you are, it'll be easier to handle and accommodate the changes swirling around you. Easier said than done, but you have to start somewhere, right? Also, just being *aware* that this constant change is a pretty standard part of the college experience helps: *Everybody* feels like they've been swept up into a weird hurricane of constant

Ask An Expert

Being Transparent About Our Struggles

"Some of the best community service college women can do is to admit to struggles and challenges and make it safe for other people to do that, too. I can't tell you how often I hear from first years who truly believe they are the only person struggling. There's so much pressure to be having the perfect experience because you've been working toward college forever, so if you're not having a great time you feel like a failure and a fraud. But everybody—even people who love college—experience those feelings at least sometimes, so it's community service to admit to it."

—Jessica Cannon, Coordinator for Health Promotion & Education for Barnard College's Wellness Center, Well Woman transition. Once you realize it's not personal, it usually becomes easier to handle.

But beyond these specific triggers, the bottom line is college is just, well, A LOT. It's super easy to feel overwhelmed for no specific reason at all. If you start to feel like the world is closing in on you (or some lesser degree of that extreme), here are my top tips for keeping your feet on solid ground:

◊ **Take care of your physical health:** Refer to all of the prior nutrition tips because, as I already mentioned, eating well, exercising, and sleeping are all *incredibly important*, not just for trying to prevent your body from becoming a decrepit shell of your comparatively robust high school self, but also for ensuring your emotional well-being. Also, drink a ton of water. I used to barely drink water at all (because, you know, coffee is a thing that exists) and, intrigued by the many students who carried around and were constantly filling up water bottles, I attempted to drink the designated 64 ounces a day and it *changed my life*. I kid you not—most of us are walking around dehydrated and wondering why we feel crappy. Drink water! It's SO EASY and you'll feel SO GREAT! You're welcome in advance.

◊ **Designate at *least* a half hour daily for YOU time:** College students often divide their time into working or socializing and almost accidentally omit designating time to one of the most restorative things they can do: having some alone time. Seriously, every day do something that is just for you, something that makes you feel whole and personally taken care of. Whether it's baking yourself some cookies, going for a run, or reading a nonschool book—whatever. Just take time to take care of yourself.

◊ **Learn who you are:** This is incredibly broad, but the bottom line is that if you know what you want, if you know what truly makes you happy and do your best to ignore what others think of you and whether or not others are judging you based on your decisions, then you will feel so much better on *every* plane of your existence. I promise you that.

DEPRESSION

Many college freshmen are disappointed to find that on a day-to-day basis, being an undergrad isn't necessarily the manically ecstatic experience society and the media are committed to insisting it is. There are as many happy and joyous occasions (hooking up without worrying about your younger sibling walking in on you, taco day in the dining hall) as there are stressful and even disconcerting moments (your first major exam, feeling like you'll never find another best friend). But although for most students these experiences even out into a feeling of basic contentment, others may begin to develop some persistent feelings of sadness and/or anxiety. Maybe it's a feeling you've had before that seems newly augmented and somewhat uncontrollable, or maybe it's a completely novel (and thus, pretty scary) experience. Either way, it's possible that these aren't just isolated feelings, but depression.

Although there doesn't seem to be a ton of transparency about it, feeling depressed is actually a pretty common experience among college-aged students. In fact, half of all college students will feel depressed at some point during their college experience (Burnsed, 2010). There is no single understanding of depression—its myriad causes and symptoms vary depending on the individual who experiences them—but here are some common symptoms according to the organization Half of Us (n.d.):

◊ persistent sadness, anxiety, irritability, or feeling of emptiness;

◊ feelings of worthlessness or hopelessness;

◊ loss of interest in previously enjoyable activities;

◊ withdrawal from friends and family;

◇ change in sleeping pattern (sleeping too much or not enough); and

◇ change in appetite and/or weight.

Although depression is a medical condition that can be genetic in origin, your environment also impacts your risk for depression, including stresses that are especially relevant to college students like living away from family for the first time, feeling overwhelmed by a complete change in routine and lifestyle, feeling alone, worrying about finances, and feeling stress generally (about work, life, the state of our economy, etc.; National Institute of Mental Health, n.d.).

So what should you do if you feel this way? First and foremost, talk to somebody about it. It's hard to believe that there are people out there who can actually help you when you feel overwhelmingly depressed and hopeless, but there really are. Chances are, your campus has resources specifically designed to help depressed students (and you can narrow in on those resources by visiting http://www.halfofus.com/find-help-now). You can also call a hotline like the National Suicide Prevention Helpline (1-800-273-TALK or 1-800-273-8255).

If you notice that a friend is exhibiting symptoms of depression, the key thing to remember is that you should in no way ignore or enable those symptoms. If you truly think your friend is struggling with depression, don't make excuses for why she missed obligations or encourage her to do things that'll interfere with her mental health (like drinking). If you are truly concerned about her, you should first try to talk to her about it. Let her know that there are absolutely things she can do that will help her feel better and she needs to reach out to a professional. If she rebuffs you or refuses to get help, it's really important to try to keep talking to her or, eventually, get her the help she needs but won't get. Many people feel like they're going behind their friend's back by doing so but, in reality, you could be saving her life.

Basically, the thing to remember is that—like most of the struggles you may experience in college—depression is not a personal failing or your individual downfall. It's something that happens to HALF of all college students and there are real, effective ways to get help. There is no shame in reaching out to any of the aforementioned resources or even a trusted friend or family member—in fact, it may just be the best thing you can do for yourself.

Out of the Mouths of ~~Babes~~ Current College Students

Depression

"Engineering at Case causes stress that makes us do weird and sad things. I was incredibly lonely and probably depressed first semester. Stress messes with you in ways you can't change, but I personally knew I couldn't get rid of all my stress and still accomplish my goals. I started doing yoga and spending at least an hour of chill time every day. Schedule relaxation time every day but also make sure you're working hard when you aren't relaxing. It's hard to draw the line between work and chill time, but do it. Schedule it. The stress from procrastination and lack of focus will make you miserable and could literally kill you."
—Ellie, Case Western Reserve University

SEXUAL HEALTH

Let's be honest: One of the strongest associations people have with college is sexual freedom. So many people think of college as an extended free-for-all orgy, a string of casual hook ups, a monogamy-free island of deviance. I (predictably) have a few thoughts on this.

First of all, college isn't exactly a cesspool of casual, carefree, never-ending sex. In fact, statistics show that *most* college students aren't hooking up with the type of frequency the outside world thinks they are, if they're hooking up at *all* (which, again, many are not). Even among those who do hook up regularly (however you choose to define that expressly ambiguous term), there are still plenty of students out there who prefer (and successfully have) long-term relationships, and even those who are perfectly happy remaining abstinent (permanently or temporarily) and everything in between. There's hardly a single sexual profile that can be applied to all college students.

Secondly, I think most people would be surprised by what way too many freshwomen *don't* know about sex (big shout out to abstinence-only sex education on this one!). Freshmen enter college with a huge range of sexual experience, knowledge, and cultural messaging that undoubtedly shapes their experiences at school and determines with whom, how, and how often they hook up. So, again, there's no single sexual profile of the average college student.

Finally—and this is specifically where this section of this chapter comes in—there's a lot of sexual health-related information women *need* to know before they enter college. Some topics are fun to talk about (enthusiastic consent, masturbation, etc.) and some are really difficult (the upsetting prevalence of abusive relationships and sexual assault on all college campuses across this country, for instance). But it's important that we cover the good *and* the bad: Knowledge is power and the more you know about sex—in terms of your own sexual health and the sex-related obstacles you might encounter—the better you'll be able to make choices and design experiences that are right for you.

THE GOOD: TAKING CONTROL OF YOUR SEXUAL HEALTH

Nothing would make me happier than having the ability to sit you all down and take you through some basic comprehensive sex ed. We'd laugh, we'd cringe, we'd awkwardly start eating a banana intended for . . . other purposes. It would be A HOOT AND A HALF. Unfortunately, I don't have the time or space to do that (although, luckily, a bunch of far more competent people did and do—check out the resources included in this section for

quite a few different types of the pill and you should consult with your primary care doctor or gynecologist about which is right for you.

☛ *Cons:* You're supposed to take the pill at the same time every day . . . which can be challenging for busy college students. But that's what smartphone alarms are for, right? The pill can also have some serious side effects for some, including (somewhat ironically) decreased sexual desire, weight gain, and/or increased depression and/or anxiety. But, then again, as the host of one of my favorite web series, the *Midwestern Teen Sex Show*, says, "[The pill] may have side effects, but so does pregnancy."

WHAT IS PLAN B?
HINT: IT'S NOT THE ABORTION PILL

Plan B tends to get a bad rap in the media and there seems to be a lot of confusion about what it is. Here are the facts:

- ◆ **WHO should use it:** Anybody whose birth control failed or wasn't used during sex and wants to avoid pregnancy.
- ◆ **WHAT it is:** Emergency contraception, which is not equivalent to an abortion, made from a one-time dose of a higher level of hormone your body makes naturally.
- ◆ **HOW it works:** These pills contain a hormone called levonorgestrel, which prevents pregnancy by delaying ovulation (the egg and sperm never meet up). Therefore, to reiterate, it has no effect on an established pregnancy and is not effective if a woman has already ovulated. You must take the actual pill within 72 hours after unprotected sex.
- ◆ **WHEN you should feel ashamed about using it:** NEVER. Look, there are wildly misguided people out there who have (generally ignorant) opinions about things like Plan B and might try to make you feel bad about using it. But it's *your* life and plenty of women fought for your right to make these types of decisions so that you *can* have the life you want. Take advantage of it and know in your heart you did the best thing for you.

◇ Intrauterine devices:

☞ *Pros:* If you feel that you're going to be sexually active for the next few years of your life and don't plan on getting pregnant during that time, getting an IUD is *absolutely* the way to go. IUDs are small devices inserted into your uterus by a sexual healthcare provider and remain there for a number of years. There are two types of IUDs: hormonal, which release the hormone levonorgestrel and last for at least 5 years, and nonhormonal, which are made of copper and can stay in place for at least 10 years. Both interfere with sperm mobility and egg fertilization to prevent pregnancy and are 99+% effective with perfect *and* typical use. You should discuss the details with your health care provider, but basically IUDs are an awesome option.

☞ *Cons:* The biggest con associated with IUDs is the fact that, like the pill, they *don't prevent STIs.* You have to use them with a barrier method (like condoms) in order to prevent disease transmission. Also, in case there are any complications at any time during the IUD's residency in your uterus, you will need to have access to an adequate health care provider who can help out. There's also a relatively high cost of insertion.

Sidenote about birth control. Ladies, if you're sexually active and use a method that is applied immediately before sex, you should carry it around with you at all times just in case. Many girls are afraid this will make them look "slutty" but seriously, screw that. Anybody who thinks that is a slut-shaming jerk and isn't worth your time. Safety first, always.

Also, these are just a few of your options. There are plenty of other methods of birth control, and if none of the above methods seem right for you, make sure to check out websites like Scarleteen and Bedsider (see p. 98). Both have amazing comprehensive descriptions and tools to help you decide what form of birth control is right for you. You can (and probably should) also visit your health center or, better yet, a gynecologist for solid advice and resources.

But although having the technical aspects of safe sex down is super important, there are some more nuanced things to remember about having safe sex generally. Here are your essential keys to safe sex:

◊ If you're having sex with dudes:
   ☛ You should be using two methods of birth control at any given time: ideally, a barrier method (method that

THE TRUTH ABOUT STIS

The traditional sex ed approach to STIs seems to be to break out a bunch of terrifying, close-up clinical photos of sexually transmitted infections that will force you to wake up sobbing when they randomly appear in an otherwise satisfying dream starring you and Ryan Gosling in a compromising position. Yet, I've found that even viewing such graphic pictures is ultimately a meager source of competition for the formidable force of nature that is adolescent hormones. So, instead, I'm just going to give you a run down of the three most common STIs (according to MTV's surprisingly great website, "It's Your (Sex) Life"). Hopefully you'll get the picture and be smart enough to try to avoid them with the aforementioned methods of contraception. I've also included pop-culture references to each disease in a last ditch effort to make this otherwise kind of horrifying section more fun. You're welcome.

CHLAMYDIA

What's the deal? Chlamydia is a genital, anal, or throat bacterial infection and also happens to be the most common STI. More than one million cases are reported annually, and young women aged 15–24 are the most affected group (It's Your (Sex) Life, n.d.). There are often no symptoms, but symptoms can involve yellow-green vaginal discharge, bleeding between periods, and/or burning during urination (lovely, right?). Chlamydia can be treated with oral antibiotics, but the disease increases the risk for other infections like pelvic inflammatory disease (which can cause infertility).

Pop-culture reference: "At your age, you're going to have a lot of urges. You're going to want to take off your clothes, and touch each other. But if you do touch each other, you will get chlamydia . . . and die." —Coach Carr, *Mean Girls*

continues

prevents sperm from entering the uterus and protects against STIs—like condoms) as well as a hormonal method (which prevents pregnancy, like the pill or IUD).

☞ You really shouldn't use methods like the "Pull Out"/"Pull and Pray"/"Withdrawal Method," which is only 78% effective with typical use. Although it's *possible* for this method to be effective, it only is if the male partner has some exceptional self-control and, ideally, if you're tracking your menstrual cycle and know when you're ovulating. Let's face it, neither are exactly characteristic of college students.

THE TRUTH ABOUT STIS, CONTINUED

HPV
What's the deal? More than 50% of sexually active people will get HPV at some point (an estimated 6 million new cases occur every year and 20 million people are already infected; It's Your (Sex) Life, n.d.). It can cause genital warts or small bumps that appear within weeks or months after being infected. There are more than 40 types of HPV, some of which can cause cancers like cervical cancer if left untreated. However, there are treatments—like freezing warts, topical medicines—and even an HPV vaccine.

Pop-culture reference: "It's Lil Poundcake, the sweetest doll on the block! . . . She has a purse and hair that grows! She'll keep you safe from HPV! . . . Lil Poundcake is the first doll approved to administer the Human Papilloma Virus vaccination to girls under 10! . . . Lil Poundcake protects against HPV, with a series of three injections over a period of 6 months! AND . . . she's got her own PHONE!" —SNL parody commercial for "Lil Poundcake" the HPV Vaccine Doll

HERPES
What's the deal? Herpes is a viral infection of the genitals (Herpes 2) and/or mouth and lips (Herpes 1) transmitted through any type of sex as well as skin-to-skin contact. About 1 in 6 people have herpes and most people don't have any symptoms other than sores (which occur during outbreaks). Medications exist to help treat symptoms and reduce frequency of outbreak and spreading it, but there is no cure.

Pop-culture reference: "You know, for me trophies are like herpes. You can try to get rid of them but they just keep coming. You know why? Sue Sylvester has hourly flair ups of burning itchy highly contagious talent." —Sue Sylvester, *Glee*

◇ If you're having sex with anybody:

☞ I have to mention that despite how I feel about abstinence-only sex education (hint: I'm not a fan), abstaining from sex *is* the only 100% fail-proof method for not getting pregnant or STIs. It's totally realistic for some and completely unrealistic for others. If you know that it's unrealistic for you, be honest with yourself and figure out the best way to regularly protect yourself.

☞ If you are sexually active, get tested for STIs regularly. Even if you're super careful and safe, you owe it to yourself and your partner(s) to be 100% sure about your sexual health. Many college health centers provide testing, as do Planned Parenthoods and other health centers across the country.

☞ You should always be in charge of your *own* sexual health. As distrustful as it sounds, never rely on your partner to provide protection. It's literally your future and you owe it to yourself to exercise the control you have over it and not allow *any* element of chance to enter the picture.

SEXUAL HEALTH RESOURCES

To learn more about how to sexually empower and care for yourself, check out these online resources. Also, consider making an appointment with a gynecologist or visiting a Planned Parenthood or other women's health care center before you leave for college. After all, they're the real professionals—I'm just a college student with a passion for sharing empowering information.

♦ **Scarleteen** (http://scarleteen.com)**:** Scarleteen, which has been offering young adults advice about sex, sexual health, sexuality, and relationships since 1998, covers every one of these topics in a thoughtful, honest, and comprehensive way. If you've ever had any (and I do mean *any*) questions about sex, your body, and beyond, Scarleteen is the website to check out.

♦ **Bedsider** (http://bedsider.org)**:** Bedsider is your one-stop shop for in-depth information about birth control. It offers a "method explorer" tool that allows you to explore and compare *every* type of birth control—from the perspectives of "most effective," "party ready," "STI prevention," "easy to hide," and "do me now"—and addresses any questions you may have about each method. It also directs you to places where you can get each method and also has an array of fun and informative articles.

♦ **Planned Parenthood** (http://www.plannedparenthood.org): Planned Parenthood is the old standby and a godsend to millions of women. Its website offers a ton of incredibly useful information about sexual health—ranging from information about abortion, birth control, relationships, sex and sexuality, STIs, women's health, and beyond. They are probably best known for their physical centers, which although they are notorious as abortion providers, also offer an amazing array of general health services that are actually affordable for all women.

Sexual empowerment. Okay, "sexual empowerment" might not be included in most comprehensive sex education programs but it *should be*. Basically, women have been subjected to oppressive cultural forces that have sought to control our bodies and reproductive rights as well as our sexual autonomy for literally centuries. When the birth control pill was approved for contraceptive use in 1960, it quite literally transformed women's lives. Women gained the unprecedented ability to control their reproductive systems and *plan* pregnancies, therefore delaying marriage and enabling them to make *autonomous decisions*. We've come a long way since that point (and arguably because of it), but unfortunately the restrictive, shaming culture that dictates women remain "pure" and "chaste" that existed for centuries before the pill and the sexual revolution is still ingrained in our society.

It's these archaic ideas about women's sexuality that tend to make true sexual empowerment difficult. They're the forces that allow bullshit double standards about women and sex to persist. For example, college women frequently encounter the "slut/whore" dichotomy that simultaneously pressures women to be always sexually appealing and available yet also dictates that if they sleep around *too* much ("too much" being a pretty arbitrary amount), then they're sluts. Under the power of this double standard, women are considered weird if they're not sexually active enough (and are "virgin shamed"), but considered whores if they're *too* sexually active (and are "slut shamed"). Women can't win under this ridiculous dichotomy of women's sexuality, which has nothing to do with our own pleasure or satisfaction and everything to do with limiting and oppressing us.

To destroy this double standard, women need to be vigilant about speaking out against it when they see evidence of it—when a guy *or* girl calls another girl a "slut" or "whore" based on the way she expresses her sexuality, when somebody pressures a girl to be sexually active when she has chosen to be abstinent, etc. But although that societal shift may take time, on a personal level you can try to overcome that double standard by acknowledging that everybody has different levels of sexual experiences, comfort, and ways of expressing their sexuality—and that it's *all* good.

But even beyond the ideological shift that needs to happen, there are a few things you can actually *do* to claim your sexual empowerment, like masturbation. There's this weirdly pervasive myth out there that only guys masturbate. There are also some ridiculously archaic myths that masturbation is THE DEVIL'S WORK and can make you blind or crazy or damage your genitals. Oh, the ignorance! The truth is that women can and do masturbate as well—and for plenty of good reasons, like:

1. **It's healthy:** Masturbation releases stress and physical tension. Orgasms can actually act as a natural painkiller and many women masturbate (and are told to masturbate by doctors, no less) to ease menstrual cramps and/or back pain (Planned Parenthood, 2013).

2. **It's an awesome way to exercise your sexual autonomy and exploration.** Want to have an orgasm without worrying about STIs or pregnancy? Hi, masturbation. One study also showed that women who masturbate have higher self-esteem than those who don't (Planned Parenthood, 2013). It makes sense: Masturbating is literally the physical act of loving yourself, a basic concept women should

wholeheartedly embrace in every aspect of our lives. Masturbating can enable you to take control of your sexuality in a really satisfying and beneficial way.

3. **Bettering sex with others.** Masturbating allows you to really get to know your body—what turns you on, what feels good. Instead of putting all the pressure on your partner to please you, knowing your body allows you to take control. If you know what you like, you'll be able to communicate it to your partner and have awesome sex. Win-win.

Before my freshman year, I expected college to be one of the few institutions in our deeply sexist country where progressive thought flourishes and yet my first year at college felt like the volume was turned way up on the speakers of sexism—especially as it related to the way women were viewed as sexual objects. Contrary to dominant depictions of college as a liberal, enlightened environment, it's often one in which highly gendered and sexist stereotypes are perpetuated. I was completely taken aback by the intensity with which not just sexism and close-mindedness related to sex and sexuality persists, but the intensity with which all types of sexism actually increased in college, in which gender stereotypes were amplified, and again, how this sexism was constantly inscribed on women's bodies.

But, although this is a persistent reality on many college campuses (and can feed into some really ugly realities of sexual violence that we'll discuss on the next page), it's also *more* than possible to claim your sexuality. Part of college is figuring out who you are—what you want, what you need, and feeling empowered to go after it, and that certainly relates to your body and sexuality as much as it does your mind.

SEXUAL EMPOWERMENT RESOURCES

Yes Means Yes!: This volume of 27 essays (edited by Jaclyn Freedman and Jessica Valenti) promotes a genuine understanding and respect for female sexual pleasure by reframing the common "No Means No" anti-rape campaign—the general negative approach to women's sexuality—by positing that instead we should celebrate women's sexual autonomy.

What You Really, Really Want: Jaclyn Freedman's awesome book on female sexual empowerment essentially answers the question: "Given all the conflicting messages young women get about their sexuality, how do they figure out what they—you guessed it—really, really want?" This book is an absolute *must-read* for any woman who wants to really explore and own her sexuality (so, all of us).

Sex+ and Laci Green (http://lacigreen.tv/): Laci Green is a blogger and vlogger in her 20s who hosts a biweekly video series and weekly live show. She also writes a daily blog, runs a peer education network and lectures at colleges across the country. To Green (n.d.), sexuality is "not just about sex" but is also "a way to connect with others, to connect with ourselves and . . . [is] also tied to more social ills than one might realize" (para. 8). Also, she's awesome and hilarious.

The Purity Myth: Valenti takes on the U.S.'s cultural tendency to place women's worth entirely on their sexuality and argues that women should be valued less for their sexuality (or purity) and more for values like honesty, kindness, and altruism.

THE BAD AND UGLY: ABUSIVE RELATIONSHIPS AND SEXUAL ASSAULT

I find it repulsive how little information incoming freshmen are presented with in terms of the nastier things they might encounter with regard to sex and sexual relationships. Whether it's because colleges want to cover up incidents of sexual assault that make them look bad (as so many do) or because they think it's "inappropriate" to get into topics that are difficult to address, the fact remains that occurrences like abusive relationships and sexual assault are by no means a college-specific phenomenon, but they *do* happen at colleges across the country—at alarming rates, no less. There are plenty of other issues we could get into here (and I will certainly direct you to other resources that address those issues), but two (unfortunately) incredibly prevalent issues that I'll address here are abusive relationships and sexual assault.

Abusive relationships. Here are the facts:

◊ 43% of college women report abusive dating behavior (including physical, sexual, technological, verbal, or controlling abuse; Love Is Respect, 2011).

◊ Nearly 1 in 3 college women say they've been in an abusive dating relationship (Love Is Respect, 2011).

◊ In one year, more than 13% of college women indicated they had been stalked and, of those, 42% had been stalked by a boyfriend or ex-boyfriend (Break the Cycle, 2011).

What is an abusive relationship? Any pattern of behavior in a dating relationship that is meant to isolate and control a partner is considered abusive (Break the Cycle, 2011). It can include:

◊ physical abuse (punching, slapping);

◊ sexual abuse (rape, sexual assault);

◊ verbal abuse (put-downs, other verbal attacks);

◊ emotional abuse (extreme jealousy, possessiveness, controlling behavior); and

◊ technological abuse (reading your text messages, calling incessantly when you're not together).

Abusive relationships aren't relegated to a certain population or a certain type of couple—it doesn't distinguish between race, religion, age, sexual orientation, etc. They can affect anyone and take the form of a *pattern* (if it happens once, chances are it's not an isolated incident and will happen again) as well as a *cycle* of power and control that looks something like Figure 2.

There is no designated starting point for this cycle and one can be in an abusive relationship without meeting every single point mentioned, but each category generally includes the tactics of abuse shown in Figure 3.

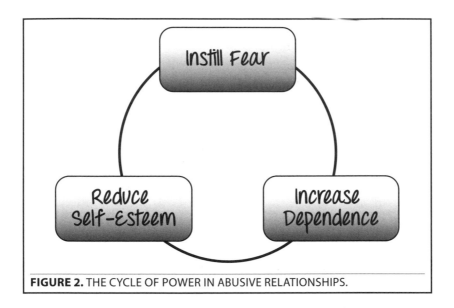

FIGURE 2. THE CYCLE OF POWER IN ABUSIVE RELATIONSHIPS.

Being a bystander. Although many people think abuse is a "private" matter restricted to just the two people in an abusive relationship, the truth is that abusive relationships impact (at least) three people (and usually more): the abuser, the target, and the bystander. Although abuse isn't always obvious to outsiders, there are plenty of instances where people will witness somebody physically, verbally, or sexually abusing someone else and do absolutely nothing about it. In fact, people are *less* likely to interfere if they feel the two people involved in a confrontation know each other and are in a relationship. Despite having the power to help—despite the fact that they may be the victim's *only* chance for help—most people won't do anything.

Why? Bystanders often feel it "isn't their place" to intervene or because they're worried that it will be a difficult and uncomfortable situation for *them*. Well, guess what? Those aren't excuses for intelligent and compassionate humans. Yes, being socially awkward sucks. Yes, inserting yourself into a situation that doesn't directly involve you can be challenging. But what sucks even more is feeling like you could have prevented or intervened in domestic abuse,

Instill Fear

- **Threats and Rumors:** The abuser may threaten to harm him- or herself, others, or the target as a means of controlling him or her. The abuser may threaten to kill him- or herself, expose secrets, spread rumors about, or send/post inappropriate pictures of the target to others should he or she try to leave or get help.
- **Intimidation and Physical Violence:** The abuser may physically assault his or her target, throw things at him or her, or intimidate him or her by driving recklessly or shouting.
- **Stalking:** About 3.4 million people over the age of 18 are stalked each year in the U.S. and 30% of stalking victims are stalked by a current or former intimate partner (U.S. Department of Justice, 2009). Constant texting/calling/e-mailing when partners are apart, or insisting to accompany a partner everywhere or showing up uninvited all qualify as stalking, especially if the behavior continues after a relationship ends. Although abusers may claim to be "looking out for" their current/former partner, they are in fact violating their partner's privacy and attempting to control them.

Increase Dependence

- **Violation of Personal Space:** The abuser may engage in unwanted physical contact or violating virtual privacy by hacking into e-mail or social media accounts.
- **Isolation:** The abuser prohibits his or her partner from seeing or spending time with anybody outside the relationship—especially those the abuser may feel intimidated by (such as another potential partner). A common defense is that "Jealousy is a sign of love" but in this case it's actually a sign of abuse.
- **Testing:** The abuser constantly tries to "test" how much the target loves him or her, such as limiting free time only to spending time together and engaging in undesired sexual acts. Abusers who test their targets often use phrases like "If you loved me you would . . ." and sometimes create alternate online profiles to test their target's online activity (and fidelity).

Reduce Self-Esteem

- **Limiting Self-Expression:** Because of their abuser's controlling behavior, targets of abusive relationships are limited by their inability to join clubs or other groups, having their free time dictated or limited, being told how they should dress or how much make-up they should wear (especially being slut-shamed for their choices), and even what types of birth control they should (or shouldn't) use. Essentially, the abused are asked to give up what they want and need in the name of what their abusers want.
- **Emotional Abuse:** Emotional abuse includes putting down somebody (i.e., telling a partner that they dress like a slut, are overweight and/or stupid, etc.) and making him or her feel guilty for what his or her abuser sees as faults, which reflect poorly on the abuser. On the other hand, abusers will often make grandiose and manipulative statements like, "You are the only person for me" or "I can never love anyone the way I love you"—used to make the abused person feel emotionally connected to the abuser.

FIGURE 3. TACTICS OF ABUSE.

could have possibly provided the help somebody so desperately needed, and just didn't. What sucks the worst is that somebody in an abusive relationship, who really needed a bystander to intervene, to reach out, is met with complete silence and nonaction.

So how can you be more than a bystander? The Ending Violence Association of British Columbia (n.d.) has some ideas:

◊ If you don't know the target:

- ☛ Most obviously you can refuse to *participate* in or encourage any kind of abusive behavior.
- ☛ If you see that somebody else is being targeted, you can stand near him or her so that the harasser or abuser knows he or she is being monitored.
- ☛ You can directly ask the person you suspect is the target of abuse if he or she is okay or if there's any way you can help.
- ☛ You can vocally address the harasser or abuser by telling him or her to stop and warning that you will call the police if he or she doesn't.

◊ If the target is a friend:

- ☛ Talk to your friend. Tell her you're aware of the abuse, are concerned, and want to help. Emphasize that it's not her fault, that she doesn't deserve it, and that she isn't alone. Avoid any judgment and don't confront your friend during an episode of violence, as you could be putting yourself in a dangerous position as well.
- ☛ Help her develop a plan. Only if she is willing, direct her to resources (like the ones listed below) and offer to help her go to the police or to a campus counselor or health center. For a more detailed plan, visit the National Coalition Against Domestic Violence website (http://ncadv.org) or check out the American Bar Association's Domestic Violence Safety Plan (http://americanbar.org/groups/domestic_violence).

☛ Recognize your limitations. The cycle of violence is really physically, emotionally, and psychologically intense. As frustrating as it may be, there may be instances where a friend is clearly in an abusive relationship but feels incapable of leaving. You have to recognize this and do everything you can to encourage your friend to get help and make yourself always available to help her, but at the end of the day you may not be able to completely convince your friend to get help, or that she's in an abusive relationship at all.

How You Can Get Help

Resources for Abusive Relationships

These organizations and websites can offer you far more information and direct plans for action. If you or somebody you know is in an abusive relationship, don't hesitate to check in with these resources as soon as you can.

♦ **Love Is Not Abuse** (http://loveisnotabuse.com and http://www.breakthecycle.org): Through its educational program "Break The Cycle," Love Is Not Abuse offers research, educational curriculum, and resources to prevent and end dating abuse specifically among young people. There is a teen-specific National Dating Abuse Helpline offered by this organization: 1-866-331-9474.

♦ **National Network to End Domestic Violence** (NNEDV; http://www.nnedv.org): NNEDV focuses on social change and aims to create an environment in which violence no longer exists through making domestic violence a national priority, changing society's interaction with domestic violence, and strengthening domestic violence advocacy.

♦ **The National Domestic Violence Hotline** (http://www.thehotline.org): First and foremost, the number to call is 1-800-799-7233, but this website also has guides for how to help friends and family in abusive relationships, survivors, how to find your own path to safety, as well as a guide to getting help for the abusers themselves.

Sexual assault and rape. I'll be really honest: This was by far the hardest part of this book to write. I personally have never been sexually assaulted but I know many—far too many—women who have been, while in college as well as at other times in their lives. The truth is, sexual assault and rape are *far* more common than a lot of women realize—like disgustingly, horrifyingly common. It's a huge issue for us (and I do mean all of us—this involves women *and* men, as perpetrators *and* as victims) as a society, as well as an issue that really is especially relevant during your time at school.

This is a critical period in our lives: Women between the ages of 16 and 24—regardless of whether or not they are students—experience rape at a rate four times higher than the general assault rate of all women (Sampson, 2002). But the college environment is *hardly* a safe-haven from sexual assault—if anything, it might be the opposite: As many as 1 in 4 women in higher educational institutions will be the victims of completed or attempted rape and yet as many as 95% of campus rapes are never reported (Fisher, Cullen, & Turner, 2000). Despite this high rate of underreporting the crime, 51% of college males *admit* to perpetrating one or more sexual assault incidents during college (Berkowitz, 1992). And this is especially relevant for freshmen to be aware of: Studies show that freshmen and sophomores are at a greater risk than juniors or seniors (Krebs, Lindquist, Warner, Fisher, & Martin, 2009).

Defining key terms. Just to be clear going forward, let's define some key terms (according to the definitions provided by RAINN—the Rape, Abuse and Incest National Network). Also important to note: Every state has a different *legal* definition for "sexual assault," as opposed to "rape"—some states use the terms interchangeably, others don't.

◊ **Rape:** "forced sexual intercourse, including vaginal, anal, or oral penetration. Penetration may be by a body part or an object" (RAINN, 2009a, para. 2)

◊ **Sexual Assault:** "unwanted sexual contact that stops short of rape or attempted rape. This includes sexual touching and fondling" (RAINN, 2009c, para. 2)

It's also important to note that both rape and sexual assault are **nonconsensual**. Consent —when both parties agree to the act—is the key to what differentiates "sex" from "rape" or "sexual assault."

What you need to know. Young women are trained to believe that sexual assault or rape happens in dark alleys to girls who are "wasted" or look "slutty" by nefarious strangers. Basically every part of that sentence is hardly true (and is all kinds of messed up), so let's take a second to unpack it and discuss what sexual assault is more likely to look like.

1. **The perpetrator:** A whopping 90% of rape victims know the person who sexually assaulted them (American Association of University Women, n.d.). The bottom line is, rape is rape: It is forced sexual intercourse. It has nothing to do with whether or not the two people are in a relationship, how long they've known each other or anything else. The act stands alone. And unfortunately, it's an act that perpetrators often get away with—97% of rapists never serve time for their crime (RAINN, 2009b).

2. **The "victim":** First and foremost, we need to address that calling somebody who has been raped a "victim" only revictimizes him or her. People who have been raped usually prefer to be called "survivors." It's not just a stronger word with more agency, but one that is in a way more accurate. They survived something that was done to them, that they had no control over, but they deserve to be defined by more than that single incident. They shouldn't be qualified by things that have happened to them, but by the things that they have done and continue to do. Calling somebody a "victim" perpetually frames her (or him—it's important to remember that 10% of survivors of sexual assault in the United States are men) as the disempowered object of that act (RAINN, 2009a). Secondly, we need to talk about victim blaming. Our culture is beyond horrible about this: When survivors speak out, if they are women, then the

knee-jerk reaction seems to be to doubt them, to ask what they were wearing, if they did anything to cause it. They are blamed for the horrifying, traumatic experience that was forced on them, which is a horrible experience in and of itself, but also often prevents them from speaking out further, from prosecuting their rapist. The knowledge of such victim-blaming keeps many women from telling anybody about the rape at all, which is problematic in terms of justice but also in terms of practicality: The majority of rapes that happen within closed communities (like college campuses) are committed by serial rapists (Lisak & Miller, 2002). So for every woman who feels that she will be shamed for exposing her rapist or won't be believed at all, that's another potential rape to occur down the line. As for men, we live in a culture that for myriad reasons—such as hypermasculinity standards, for example—seems to try to deny and/or erase the reality of male survivors of sexual assault and/or violence. Thus, men often don't speak out, either. Bottom line: It's essential to put blame not on the person who was raped but on the *rapist*—where it belongs. We don't need to teach people how to *prevent* rape—(especially in terms of what women specifically wear and how much they should drink). We need to teach *rapists* not to rape in the first place.

A really key part of changing the conversation surrounding rape and rape culture generally is to change the conception that people (especially women) should constantly be on guard and policing their partners by telling them "no," to the idea that both partners should only proceed if they hear a (enthusiastic!) *yes*. This is known as "enthusiastic consent" and is at the heart of any healthy approach to a sexual relationship . . . and yet it's not exactly something taught in sex ed across the country (or in the cultural zeitgeist generally). Yet there are *so* many benefits to promoting enthusiastic consent, like:

◊ **Taking the burden/blame off of women:** We live in a victim-blaming culture. When women are sexually assaulted, the first question we ask is, "Well did *she* say no? What did *she* do to provoke her attacker?" Beyond being mind-numbingly infuriating that it's actually a thing to hold a person accountable for a horrible thing done *to* them, this idea perpetuates the idea that men are sexually uncontrollable and that it's women's duty to reign them in and not provoke them in any way—a notion highly insulting to women as well as men. Enthusiastic consent should be about partners making an agreement—it involves them *both*.

◊ **Making the situation very clear:** "Gray rape" is a phrase that has been circulating with regard to conversations about rape culture in recent years. The term refers to the situation in which a partner may not have specifically said "no" but didn't express consent, either. I want to be very clear: If a rape occurs, it by no means should be blamed on a woman's lack of clarity. The idea of enthusiastic consent is that *everybody* involved can be *very clear* about what they want and what they're going to do before they do it, especially and primarily men. Enthusiastic consent first and foremost teaches men to only act in terms of gaining (and continuously confirming) consent and therefore (ideally) changes the mindset with which both partners enter into a sexual encounter.

◊ **Setting the mood:** There's a pesky rumor that enthusiastic consent "kills the mood"—it takes you outside of yourself, out of the moment. But I would argue that it's actually a total turn on. You're both agreeing that *yes*, you both *really* want to have sex with each other. Also, until rape doesn't persist at a disturbingly high rate, I think the argument can be made that beyond "killing the mood," explicitly consenting—and teaching men to *only* act upon having an indication of enthusiastic consent—is just culturally necessary.

For further information check out:

◇ *The Consensual Project* (http://www.theconsensualproject. com), which works with schools and universities to help students gain a fresh perspective on consent, and

◇ *Force: Upsetting Rape Culture* (http://upsettingrapeculture. com), which aims to create a new culture of consent and honest conversations about sexual violence.

What to do if you have been sexually assaulted or raped. I hope to God you never have to use this information, but it is *essential* to know should you have to.

◇ First, if you're not sure whether or not you have been raped, RAINN has an excellent tool to help you work through the incident, which can be accessed here: http://www.rainn. org/get-information/types-of-sexual-assault/was-it-rape. However, if you feel like you were raped, it probably means you didn't consent to a sexual act, which *is* rape.

◇ Do not shower, change your clothes, or even eat, drink, wash your hands, or brush your teeth—you need to save all physical evidence of the assault. Go to the hospital, or to your campus's health center as soon as possible to receive care and have a rape kit done.

◇ Report the incident to the police as soon as possible. Report and/or write down everything you can remember about the incident.

◇ Do not keep the incident to yourself, *especially* if you think people will blame you or be ashamed of you. That's that victim-blaming mentality at play and it's this type of powerlessness that the rapist wanted you to feel. The people who love you will always love you and will want to do all that they can to help you. Do not let the incident shame you into silence.

◊ Take care of yourself. Call a rape crisis center, find a counselor, and surround yourself with loved ones. Do everything and anything possible to get the help and support you need.

How to help a friend who was sexually assaulted or raped.

◊ If you witness the actual incident, resist the bystander effect. As mentioned in the above section on dating violence, people are less likely to intervene in a situation that's between two people who know each other and especially between those they know are in a relationship, but it's always better to be safe than sorry. If you think something is wrong between two people, it's always worth risking social awkwardness to double check that everything's okay.

◊ If a friend tells you she was sexually assaulted or raped, do everything you can to convince her to take action against her rapist. There are some people who say that a rape survivor has the right to not want to deal with her rapist again—to avoid the heavy emotional process of confronting her rapist and reliving the trauma of the incident. That may be valid, but at the same time, doing nothing also has heavy consequences. On a personal level, not prosecuting your rapist does little to assuage the trauma you've already experienced and may continue to experience (like PTSD). On a greater level, as mentioned before, the majority of rapes that happen within closed communities (like college campuses) are committed by serial rapists, which means if your friend doesn't speak out, her rapist will likely rape somebody else (or even multiple others; Lisak & Miller, 2002). Speaking out may save others from having the same experience.

◊ Generally, help guide your friend through the aforementioned steps and refer to the resources below. Essentially, once you've made sure that your friend gets the help she needs and is in contact with professionals and people with more authority, your job is to be there for her. She'll need support and being able to offer it in abundance is one of the best things you can do for her.

What you need to know about Title IX and the Clery Act. There are a few college-specific pieces of legislation that enter into this picture about which far too many young women don't know. They are Title IX and the Clery Act, and they're both covered more in depth by the organization Know Your IX (http://knowyourix. org), which everybody should check out for more information. But here are the basics:

◊ **Title IX:** Most people who are familiar with Title IX think it's all about sports. The common example cited for this landmark federal civil right is that it required schools to distribute equal funding to programs for men and women— thus, the rise of women's sports teams in high schools and colleges across the country. But what most people don't realize is that it generally prohibits sex discrimination in education, including sexual harassment, gender-based discrimination, and sexual violence. It requires schools to take immediate action based on any reasonable knowledge they have about discrimination, harassment, or violence to eliminate it, remedy harm caused, and prevent its recurrence (Bolger, n.d.). Under Title IX, schools must have a Title IX Coordinator who manages an established procedure for handling complaints about such issues and is able to take actions like issuing a "no contact directive," which prevents the accused rapist from approaching or interacting with the assaulted party (Bolger, n.d.). Schools are *not* allowed to encourage or allow mediation instead of a formal hearing of the complaint (which might make them look better or allow the rapist to get off easy) and can't discourage you from continuing your education (Bolger, n.d.).

◇ **The Clery Act:** This act is, according to the Know Your IX website, "a federal law that requires colleges to report crimes that occur 'on campus' and school safety policies . . . [and] requires schools to have timely warning when there are known risks to public safety on campus" (Brinn & List, n.d., para. 1). The Clery Act also has a "Campus Sexual Assault Victim's Bill of Rights" which was also recently expanded by the Campus SaVE Act, which, together, require colleges to "disclose educational programming, campus disciplinary process, and victim rights regarding sexual violence complaints . . . [and] address all incidents of sexual violence" (Brinn & List, n.d., para. 2). This is meant to help make the process for reporting incidents, possible sanctions, mental health resources, and other rights (like your rights during a campus disciplinary proceeding) more transparent to students, as well as protects students against possible retaliation on the part of the school (like intimidating, threatening, or discriminating against you if you choose to report an incident; Brinn & List, n.d.).

For more information about Title IX generally, how to file a Title IX complaint, pursue a Title IX lawsuit, the pros and cons of filing such a complaint or pursuing a lawsuit, and the Clery Act, visit Know Your IX's website (http://knowyourix.org).

Resources. The truth is, despite Title IX, college administrations often try to cover up sexual assault incidences. In 2013 alone, USC, Occidental, Swarthmore, Berkeley, Dartmouth, Vanderbilt, and Amherst all faced federal complaints for failing to address sexual assault and harassment on campus (Kingkade, 2013; Mukherjee, 2013). A report on how Yale handles sexual misconduct found that it refuses to use the term *rape* and punishes the act with a mere "written reprimand" (Baker, 2013). The list goes on.

But this section isn't about college administrators (although you should look into it—it's important to know your school's history on this issue and it's something that NEEDS to change). It's about you and giving you the resources to best empower yourself. So although dealing with your college's resources and administration may be necessary (and, truthfully, may very well be a battle), here are other organizations and resources to help and support you.

◊ **Know Your IX** (http://knowyourix.org): This campaign "aims to educate all college students in the U.S. about their rights under Title IX." This comprehensive website and support system—which offers detailed information about Title IX and the Clery Act as well as guidance through the processes involved with both—was built by a group of survivor-activists and allies hoping to share their experiences and arm themselves with knowledge and support.

◊ **The American Association of University Women** (AAUW; http://www.aauw.org): The AAUW is also dedicated to fighting campus sexual assault through its Legal Advocacy Fund. Its website has information about sexual assault and "strategies for change." The sexual assault-specific resources can be found here: http://www.aauw.org/what-we-do/legal-resources/know-your-rights-on-campus/campus-sexual-assault/

◊ **Promoting Awareness Victim Empowerment** (PAVE; http://www.pavingtheway.net/wordpress): PAVE is a non-profit organization whose focusing principle is the tactic of shattering silence about violence and using education and social action to end sexual violence.

◊ **Rape, Abuse & Incest National Network** (RAINN; http://www.rainn.org): RAINN is the largest anti-sexual violence organization in the U.S. and along with its National Sexual Assault Hotlines—1.800.656.HOPE (phone) and online.

rainn.org (instant messaging)—the organization partners with more than 1,100 local rape crisis centers and also operates the DoD Safe Helpline for the Department of Defense. It also has an abundance of helpful resource and information on its website.

◊ **Men Can Stop Rape** (http://www.mencanstoprape.org): This organization may not be immediately helpful in terms of resources or dealing with the aftermath of sexual assault, but it sure does a lot to instill hope for the future. Men Can Stop Rape works to mobilize males to create a culture free from violence, especially men's violence against women by using their strength and hopes to prevent violence through sustained initiatives throughout the world.

◊ **Project Unbreakable** (http://project-unbreakable.org and http://projectunbreakable.tumblr.com): Again, not necessarily an informational resource, but one that may help you better understand what survivors go through and/or help you heal. Founder Grace Brown started photographing survivors of sexual assault holding a poster with a quote from their attacker in 2011 and has received more than a thousand submissions to date. The tumblr's mission is to increase awareness about the issues surrounding sexual assault and encourage the act of healing through art.

CHAPTER 5

LET'S TALK ABOUT DEBT, BABY

If you're anything like me, words like "fiscal" and "economic" and "marketplace" were always like a Muggle version of the Petrificus Totalus curse. Whenever the conversation turned to such topics, I felt my limbs slowly grow heavy, my eyes glaze over, and my mind turn to contemplating the ugly-cuteness of bulgy-eyed pugs. I never used to think much of it, content with letting myself believe that finance was just a soulless industry run by sociopathic, White, Ivy-League educated men with zero respect for women or minorities and that it had very little to do with me. And then I started the college process and woke up to the truly horrific reality of soaring college tuition, seemingly inevitable debt, and a crappy economy: the unholy financial trinity of attending college in this day and age.

I don't think I'm the only girl who was so ignorant about the nitty-gritty of financial responsibility even at the cusp of adulthood. Finance is a historically male-dominated industry, topic of conversation, concern, and responsibility. Until relatively recently, women had no access to their own money and remained completely financially dependent on men. They were passed from their fathers to their husbands, literally considered property in the eyes of the law. Women who didn't marry were considered a burden on their families and, without their families' help, were often left destitute.

Historical Perspective
Women and Finance

Because our generation was largely told we're equal to our brothers and guy friends, many of us don't realize just how recently our rights were won. Which I guess is the point: Our mothers and grandmothers fought for equality so we could make the most of it, not so we could sit around rehashing the past. But by forgetting how recently women were considered subordinate, we forget that nothing happens in a vacuum. History absolutely informs everything that happens in the present, and the way women approach money is no exception. Here are just a few reminders of how recently various economic rights were won:

♦ **The Declaration of Sentiments and Resolutions**, created at the Seneca Falls Convention in 1848, called for an end to laws that denied married women control of any money and/or property (among other things—it was actually one of the first times American women formally fought for legal, economic, and social autonomy).

♦ More than 100 years later, the **Equal Pay Act** (1963) was passed, making it illegal for men to make more money than women for equal work. It's worth noting that, despite this legislation, women still only make an estimated 77 cents to every man's dollar—a figure that's even lower for women of color (National Women's Law Center, 2013).

♦ The **Equal Credit Opportunity Act** was passed in 1974 and made it illegal for creditors to deny somebody a credit card based on gender, race, religion, marital status, etc. (Moody, 2013).

♦ Before the **Women's Business Ownership Act** passed in 1988, some states still legally required women to have a male relative cosign their loan for anything from a business to a car to a home, even if they were employed and financially qualified. Let me just emphasize that: Less than *30 years ago* women couldn't get their own loans in some places.

When reminded of this context, it's easy to see how women's financial autonomy is truly novel in our historically male-dominated society. But even in this day and age, despite having come so far from having the financial autonomy of a toaster, many (if not most) women my age are largely uneducated about finance, or at least are not encouraged to learn about it the way our male counterparts are.

The thing is, lacking financial literacy is just not acceptable for women today—from an ideological perspective of female independence, of course, but also on a very practical level rooted in women's current economic reality. Studies show that women are making great strides in gaining more financial independence: In fact, a 2013 Pew Study found that women are now the leading or only breadwinners in a whopping 40% of American households (Wang, Parker, & Taylor, 2013). And yet, despite such advancement, women often feel less confident than men in understanding financial products, their ability to make financial choices, and their understanding of their own economic standing (Malcolm, 2012).

Overcoming this lack of financial confidence and becoming more educated about how to manage money is in fact necessary for women's practical self-sufficiency and survival. As of 2013, more than 15% of women in the U.S. are divorced or separated (Bowling Green State University, 2013). It's also well known that women live longer than men—5 to 10 years longer on average (Blue, 2008). Facts like these prompted the National Center for Women and Retirement to estimate that as many as 95% of women will be solely responsible for making their own financial decisions at some point in their lives (Tascarella, 2005). Therefore, it doesn't matter if we opt to remain single and/or pursue careers or if we decide to go the traditional homemaker route: No matter what choices we make, the vast majority of us will *need* to be in control of our financial decisions for at least some period of time.

And really, all women should actively try to be financially independent and secure our entire lives no matter what choices we make for a very practical reason. At the risk of sounding like a crazy person holed up in a deserted cave in the middle of Nowhere, Montana, kept company only by my own rambling thoughts of government conspiracies and a feral squirrel named Albert Von Huffenstuff:

YOU CAN'T TRUST OR DEPEND ON ANYBODY BUT YOURSELF.

Seriously, though: Although ridiculous (and by ridiculous, I, of course, mean amazing guilty pleasure) films like *The Notebook* have indoctrinated us to believe that our partners will not only support us but do things like build us entire lakeside mansions by hand out of unwavering devotion and recount our lives together day after day to jog our Alzheimer-ridden minds, getting married in no way equates to financial security.

And I'm not the only one to assert that. Author Leslie Bennetts agrees and even wrote a whole book about it. In *The Feminine Mistake*, Bennetts argues that women *should* work even if they get married because becoming financially dependent opens women up to great vulnerability on all levels. "Women who abandon their careers and become financially dependent on their husbands often look back on that decision as the biggest mistake of their lives, even women in stable, enduring marriages," she wrote in a *Huffington Post* article about the response to her book (Bennetts, 2007, para. 3). Financial independence, Bennetts noted, gives women "power in their marriages and options in the larger world, not to mention opportunities that benefit their families" (Bennetts, 2007, para. 5). And studies back Bennetts up: They show that financial issues are the No. 1 cause for married couples' arguments and can even predict divorce rates (Rampell, 2009; Tysiac, 2012). Thus, it would appear that financial independence can only *benefit* all women—even those in long-term relationships.

But dependent romantic relationships are not the only ones to be avoided: Although it's becoming increasingly common (and acceptable) to rely on them, your parents and/or guardians are not a stable source of financial support either. Once you're a legal adult, there are no guarantees. Even if you're lucky enough to have parents capable of and willing to support you, it's entirely possible (and even likely) that Mom and/or Dad will get fed up with supporting your sorry ass on a personal level or maybe they'll face financial difficulty of their own that prohibits them from helping you. The harsh truth is, once you're an adult, your only truly reliable source of financial support is yourself.

But beyond not being able to rely on dependent relationships on a practical level, financial savvy is about making your own choices and about being your own person—a principle at the heart of the college experience, and one that is hardly better facilitated than by paying for college. Funding a college education is not just the first big financial decision most women make, but it's also one of the most impactful—in fact, it's the second largest investment most people ever make (Bissonnette, 2010). Paying for college is one of the best opportunities young women have to forge and design their own paths, to lay the foundation for the lives they want to lead. How you decide to pay for school actually has the ability to shape your entire life—for better and for much, much worse.

First, the better: Surveys show that Americans with college degrees earn 50% more than those with just high school degrees over their lives (Mathews, 2003). However, a college degree is increasingly becoming less advantageous in terms of earnings than it is necessary on the basic level of employment. A February 2013 *The New York Times* article declared that "the college degree is becoming the new high school diploma: the new minimum requirement, albeit an expensive one, for getting even the lowest-level job" (Rampell, para. 1).

And then there's the devastating and potentially life-altering reality of ill-advised and/or mismanaged student debt. More than 38 million Americans have student loan debt (Epperson, 2013). This debt has surpassed a total of more than $1 trillion (Wang et al., 2013). That's 20% of U.S. households and 40% of people younger than 35 who are currently in debt due to their education—a 200% increase over the past 20 years (Wang et al., 2013). And this problem is only getting worse: The number of student borrowers in this country is only increasing, as are tuition costs, which have risen an insane 1,120% since 1978 (Jamrisko & Kolet, 2012).

But the sheer quantity of debt isn't even the biggest problem according to experts: It's the fact that such debt is indicative of a corrupt and broken system that benefits the government but hurts individual citizens and is undeniably hurting our entire economy, which obviously impacts all of us in ways both broad and intimately personal.

So what's the best course of action? Although wishing for a Student Loan Fairy Godmother to descend from Higher Education Heaven and convert your pile of hoarded Beanie Babies and McDonald's Happy Meal toys into liquid cash is definitely one (wildly optimistic) strategy, the other is to thoroughly educate yourself about your college payment options and prudently pick the one that's best for you. Because I would never wish upon you the hell that is wading through the convoluted and boring information about student loans out there, I will now present you with this, your *Smart Girl's Guide to Paying for College Without Incurring Crippling Debt That Destroys Your Life.*

GIVE IT TO ME STRAIGHT: YOUR BASIC OPTIONS

The hard truth is that the best way to financially approach college is to start early—like much earlier than right before you head off to college. Ideally, you will have been born an heiress to the Hostess fortune (access to money and I can only presume unlimited, delicious baked goods full of hydrogenated fat—it's the dream). If you were born a mere plebe, you will have gotten straight As, cured cancer, qualified for the Olympic badminton team, saved all of the homeless puppies in your hometown, and, if you found a spare minute, perhaps won first prize in the county fair for your scrumptious apple pie (you know, on a whim). Thus, you will be a shoe-in for athletic, academic, merit, and culinary (if they exist?) scholarships and will be flush with other generous souls' cash.

If accomplishing all of those things wasn't realistic for you, first take a good, hard look at your life because you are *clearly* a hopeless failure. After you thoroughly shame yourself for failing to achieve a combination of goals that would take a gaggle of grown adults entire lifetimes to accomplish before the end of your teens, take a deep breath and consider these options.

SCHOLARSHIPS

Even if you're not the world's most perfect teen, there may still be a chance of obtaining a scholarship. Scholarships, which are by definition achievement-based grants, award students free money for being awesome. They don't require repayment and thus help you avoid debt by keeping your financial responsibilities and culpabilities to a minimum. However, scholarships don't exactly grow on trees: In fact, only 7% of undergraduate students receive scholarships from third-party organizations and the average reward is a less-than-comprehensive $1,982 (Bissonnette, 2010). College-awarded scholarships are even harder to come by: They only account for 2%–3% of all college aid awarded annually and the scholarship is often only valid for one year (Bissonnette, 2010).

But just because they may not be easy to get nor will they likely fund your entire education, I should just emphasize: FREE. MONEY. There are zero drawbacks to applying for as many scholarships as you can. Although you should ideally start applying for them during your senior year of high school (if not earlier), scholarships are offered on an ongoing basis, and because most scholarships are only valid for a single academic year anyway, there's no reason not to keep applying throughout your college career.

Here are some basic scholarship tips:

◇ **There's a scholarship out there for everybody:** Although many people believe scholarships are only available for the next Michael Jordan/LeBron James/[I don't follow sports *at all* so enter relevant talented athlete here] or the next Marie Curie/Susan Sontag/[yes I am an elderly woman], there are actually plenty of scholarships out there that have no GPA, athletic, or other requirements. If you have no hand-eye coordination or math-class-specific narcolepsy, there is hope for your college education yet.

◇ **Even small awards add up:** I know so many people who, feeling defeated by the insane amount of tuition facing them, didn't even bother applying for scholarships in the $1,000 to $5,000 range and instead focused on going for the giant, all-encompassing prizes. MISTAKE. Even if you only win a single $1,000 scholarship, that's a grand more than you had to begin with. That money could cover your books and other various fees for the year. Every cent counts.

◇ **Applying for scholarships may be time-consuming, but stick with it:** It's true—if you apply for scholarships the right way (i.e., for a ton of them consistently) it can be a really tedious and time-consuming process. Unless you reward yourself with a jellybean or gummy bear every time you finish reading or writing a paragraph of the application (a foolproof method, let me tell you), it can be all but unbearable. But there are definitely ways to beat the system. There are awesome scholarship search tools out there,

Out of the Mouths of ~~Babes~~ Current College Students

Scholarships

"A piece of advice to any high school students: Start early and apply to local scholarships. Although local ones may be more work, you have a much better chance of getting them than national scholarships. Also do not brush off the scholarships for small amounts, they add up and every little bit helps!"
—Rose, University of Oregon

like http://scholarships.com, which allows you to sort and search scholarships for maximum efficiency. And seriously, after what I'm about to tell you about your other financial options, searching through scholarship databases is going to seem like a freaking cakewalk.

WORKING

The ideal way to approach paying for college is to combine applying for *all* of the scholarships humanly possible with working your ass off—throughout high school, over summers, and while in college as well, either through a college subsidized work study program or on your own time. *But Julie*, you might be thinking to yourself, *I am just barely an adult and have few marketable skills. What am I to do to earn some meager wages?* Well, there are some classic options:

◊ **Babysitting:** It's undeniably a stereotypical choice for girls and if you have the urge to yell "CHILDREN YOUR AGE ARE DYING FROM MALARIA" every time your precious charges throw tantrums over still slightly frozen chicken nuggets, or if everything that happens on the Disney Channel makes you want to give up on humanity (obviously I'm not speaking from experience), it may not be the right option for you. But if you have that maternal gene, it's pretty easy to find work, pays well, and is under the table so you don't have to worry about losing out to taxes. Plus, if you play it right you can make the children your loyal minions (which, *of course*, I don't officially endorse).

◊ **Service industries:** It's common knowledge that if you can survive the ridiculous demands, rudeness, and sometimes straight up stupidity of customers in any type of retail or food service industry, you have developed a marketable and vital life skill. Seriously, serving people to their satisfaction is *not* easy and it's actually something future employers recognize as such and thus love to see on your résumé, because it says a lot about your character. And of course, any job where you can make tips on top of a salary is a plus. Also, in retail you usually get an employee discount, so, you know, score.

◊ **Start your own business:** Are you an expert bead crafts-woman? Do your knitted shawls rival your Amish grand-mother's? Sell them! SELL THEM ALL. With the rise of online marketplaces like Etsy and eBay (that's still a thing, right?) there are plenty of ways to make your fabulous creations widely available for purchase. Also, if you have skills that don't translate directly into a concrete product—like if you're a graphic designer, bilingual, or a real-life guitar hero—don't be afraid to market your skills. Put up ads online or ask your parents to tell their friends that you're available to tutor or redesign a website. Young women today abound with marketable skills—we're just rarely clued into the fact that we can (and should) capitalize on them.

FINANCIAL AID

I hate to break it to you, but no matter how vehemently college admissions officers swear up and down that they are need blind and will meet all demonstrated need, their definition of "demonstrated need" is not one that most reasonable human beings can get behind. The Free Application for Federal Student Aid (FAFSA) form that you submit with your college application evaluates how much aid is recommended for a school to award you for a single year. The college then uses this expected contribution to evaluate how much aid they'll give you, which could include straight up money, a work study program, or recommended loans—in fact, the average financial aid package is actually 60% loans (Bissonnette, 2010). At the end of the day, colleges are businesses that want to make a profit and/or need to service a *ton* of students who also

TO OFFER MY TIME AND LABOR FOR FREE OR NOT (THE INTERNING DEBATE)

At some point in your college career, you'll likely enter into the realm of internship panic: Suddenly, your peers seem to realize that apparently no adequate job application is complete without work experience or ~~slave labor~~ internships, which are generally unpaid opportunities to work for a company or organization in your field of interest. Most college freshmen aren't concerned with (or expected to) intern, but it's definitely something to keep in mind for the years to come—and to consider carefully.

- ◆ **Pros:** Internships allow you to explore your possible career interests, allowing you to rule out an area of work if you find you hate it, or help you narrow your academic interests toward a certain career route. Internships also open doors for later job opportunities, allowing you to make connections that may lead to a job down the road.
- ◆ **Cons:** Because they are usually unpaid, internships require you to offer a significant amount of your time (and life) for basically the vague promise of an advantage down the line. Also, most internship programs expect *very* little of their charges, allowing them to create basic Excel sheets or grab coffee, which can be really frustrating and boring.

If you decide you want to intern, check in with your campus's career resources (including a designated center/office, listserv, career fairs, or alumni networks). Also, check out specific internship-focused websites like http://idealist.org (for nonprofit opportunities), http://PRSSA.org (for PR opportunities), or http://spj.org (for journalistic opportunities).

Also make sure to value yourself and your time. Try to get a paid internship if at all possible, because you should be compensated for your time and effort. There's a lot of pressure to take any internship offered—paid or not—but just know that no matter what you decide, your work has value and there should be a limit to how much you do for free.

need money. Giving you a ton of money isn't going to help them achieve either of those goals. Therefore, there are a few basic issues with relying on (or expecting to rely on) financial aid, even if you do consider yourself financially needy.

◇ **The FAFSA form usually fails to capture the financial reality of you and/or your family:** The thing about this system is that numbers on paper hardly tell the full story of what your family can actually expect to put toward your education. It's not uncommon for schools to determine that you *technically* have enough money to pay for a certain amount of tuition every year—not taking into account the fact that your parents need to help out your grandparents, or save for your siblings' education, or *eat*, or any number of infinite financial scenarios not captured by a form. Or maybe you don't qualify for financial aid at all, but you certainly don't have the kind of money necessary to fund an entire college education lying around. Ultimately FAFSA's determination of "need" is pretty out of touch with the financial reality of many (if not most) families.

◇ **Your school might try to get you "hooked":** Let's say that miraculously you get an amazing aid package to the school of your dreams. *Huzzah*, you think to yourself, *a prosperous future is within grasp!* You attend your sickeningly expensive dream school for a fraction of the cost. You're on top of the world. Then, upon receiving your sophomore aid package, you realize it isn't quite as generous. *All right,* you think, *I'll just pick up a few extra shifts, it'll be fine.* You manage. Then your junior year comes around and you're sure there has been a clerical error: that extra 0 does *not* belong at the end of your expected contribution. How are you going to pay?

This is how some colleges hook you: They give students a solid initial financial aid package then raise your expected contribution every year. You've already invested in the school, financially and personally, so you feel obligated to make it work by taking out extra loans or doing whatever else you need to when you probably could've gotten an overall cheaper education at a different school.

Just add this to the list of ways some schools (*especially* private schools) try to screw you over. If you want to go to college and can't pay out of pocket, you'll need to jump through the financial aid hoops. Just remember to be smart and realistic about comparing packages and keep in mind that the package you're offered is only valid for a year, so even if you get a great deal at a super expensive college . . . it's still a super expensive college and there may be no guarantees for the next 3 years.

LOANS

College is actually just the beginning of a world of adult responsibilities and navigating the horrifically boring and usually demeaning and depressing world of student loans is the perfect example of that. Welcome to adulthood, lady friend! It's all downhill from here!

Student loans are like any other loans in the most basic sense: You borrow money from a lender with the understanding that you will repay what you borrowed plus interest. There are actually quite a few types of student loans (see Table 2), which is good in the sense that choices are always welcome and horrible in the sense that an overabundance of options can be really overwhelming and confusing for an 18-year-old who has no idea what's going on and can lead to some seriously bad choices.

Countless college grads have horror stories that go something like this: Feeling overwhelmed by an abundance of financial speak and lack of thorough knowledge and research, they signed on the dotted line of a loan at 18 that eventually destroyed the rest of their lives. And unfortunately that is *not* hyperbole: Misinformed borrowers have ended up unemployable, owing considerably more than the cost of their college tuition, and/or defaulting (not being able to make loan payments) and lead lives generally dictated by crippling debt—opting not to start families, unable to become homeowners or start their own businesses because of crappy credit scores, and laughing at the idea of actually following their dreams— all based on a single decision they *literally* made before their frontal lobe was fully developed.

"A high percentage of student borrowers enter into their loans having no idea that they're signing up for a relationship as unbreak-

Table 2
Types of Loans Available

Loan	Description	The Nitty Gritty
Stafford Loan	Stafford loans are the most common types of federal loan. They're capped based on the degree to which a student's financially dependent on their parents and what year you are in school. There are two types of Stafford loans: **subsidized** and **unsubsidized.**	A **subsidized Stafford loan** is determined by financial need, which is determined by your school. A common complaint is that schools have a convoluted way of calculating such need and tend to overestimate how much you and your family can realistically pay. You don't have to pay interest on the loan until a few months after graduation at a lower rate than unsubsidized. To get the **unsubsidized Stafford loan**, you don't need to demonstrate financial need—your school determines how much you can borrow based on tuition and any other financial aid you receive. However, you have to pay interest on the loan from the moment you get it.
Perkins Loan	Perkins loans are for students with extreme financial need and are capped at $27,500 for your entire undergraduate education although you may be able to receive as much $5,500 in a single year. Interest rates of this loan are a standard 5%.	Your school lends this money—meaning you will pay the school and funds available are dependent on the availability of funds at your college.
Parent PLUS Loan	This loan is issued directly to a student's parents to help with costs that are absolutely not covered by other forms of aid.	Although these loans can be helpful if your parents are willing to help you, it's not advisable for parents to risk their own financial well-being or to borrow against retirement or their 401K to finance this loan (or their child's education generally).
Consolidation Loan	Consolidation loans combine several loans into a single package by calculating a weighted average of your individual loans' rates and rounding up to the nearest 1/8 percent. The interest rate for this loan is capped at 8.25%.	The benefit to this is being able to make a single monthly payment instead of a bunch of different ones. You may also be able to lower monthly payments and might have access to different repayment plans, which could prove beneficial. Beware of losing borrower benefits from the original loan, though, which could include interest rate discounts or loan cancellation benefits.
Institutional Loan	This loan is like a scholarship in that it's offered directly by the school you're attending without involving any middlemen.	However, unlike scholarships, you still have to pay back the school once you graduate.

able as herpes," Matt Taibbi noted in a 2013 *Rolling Stone* magazine piece about student debt (p. 4). And it's true: Student loans are life-sucking bitches *designed* to encourage borrowers to default, which seems completely unjust considering that a college degree is required for most jobs, and taking out a loan is actually the only option for most people to get that degree. Ultimately, the basic path we've established for securing future financial stability is *anything but* financially secure or even in our best interest.

So how did we get into this insane situation? Well, first of all, it's worth remembering that this phenomenon is actually pretty recent: It was arguably incited when Pell grants became available to all undergrads (notably, including women and minorities) in 1976–1977, making college a realistic option for more students than ever before (Online Colleges, 2013). However, as a college education became increasingly accessible, it also became more unaffordable, which necessitated many students to take out loans, which became (possibly too) readily available. Tuition costs continue to rise: By 2029, public university tuition is predicted to rise to $41,228 and private colleges' tuition to a truly sickening $92,869 (Landsman, 2012). Student loan debt rises alongside tuition; in fact, the Class of 2013 has an average of $30,000 of student loan debt (making it the most indebted graduating class ever; Izzo, 2013).

There are myriad factors contributing to the exponential increase of both tuition and student debt, including:

◇ **The government profits from student loan debt:** The U.S. government *profits* from students who default on their loans, so the system is set up to encourage defaulting. The U.S. Department of Education makes as much as $1.22 for every defaulted dollar (Korn, 2011). Even under President Obama's new federal student loan system passed in 2013, which was said to cut out the middle man and pass savings on to students, the government will make an estimated $184 billion over 10 years (Taibbi, 2013).

◇ **Decreased state spending on education:** Since the 2008 recession, state spending on higher education has decreased an average of 28% nationwide, and schools have had to find ways to compensate for this loss (Online Colleges, 2013). And yet, despite this loss of funds, the education industry still spent $88–$110 million lobbying the government each year for the past 6 years and recklessly spends money on efforts to boost their rankings (instead of their students' financial well-being), like state of the art dorms and celebrity professors (Taibbi, 2013).

◇ **Removed consumer protections:** In order to encourage defaulting, consumer protections have been removed from student loans. For example, although declaring bankruptcy is a viable option for anybody else in debt (including gamblers, for instance) those with student loan debt can't declare bankruptcy. In fact, student debt collectors can dip into anything from a borrower's wages to their tax returns to their social security payments to, despicably, disability checks to cover student loans (Taibbi, 2013). Although other indebted individuals can refinance their loans to make payments more manageable, those with student debt aren't able to refinance. What's more (and what seriously, in my really biased opinion, is a freaking travesty), lenders are *legally allowed* to deceive teenage clients by not giving them access to information like what the interest rate on their loan will be until after they graduate and are stuck paying it (Taibbi, 2013).

◇ **Monthly wages vs. monthly fees:** Because college costs have been rising at more than two times the rate of inflation, students are taking out larger loans that result in sizeable monthly fees—and yet the monthly earnings of an average grad are hardly keeping up. In fact, 50% of those who graduated since 2008 are currently under- or unemployed (Neal, 2012). Real middle class income has stagnated over the last three decades, and some claim that middle class income has even fallen backward (Pew Research Center, 2012). What's more, the pool of college graduates is growing more than twice as fast as the pool of jobs requiring a college degree, indicating that underemployment and unemployment among college grads is only going to increase (Lubin, 2013).

These reasons contribute to the fact that one out of every five students graduating with more than $15,000 of debt *will* default within 10 years and the estimated overall default rate is a whopping 1 in 3 (Bissonnette, 2010). But, even worse, this situation affects our economy at large: A complete lack of jobs (let alone well-paying jobs) for college grads and ridiculous tuition costs that necessitate insanely high student loan payments results in one third of all student loan borrowers defaulting (hardly just an irresponsible minority). One out of every three borrowers is punished with life-altering penalties like bad credit scores that make getting any other loans (like for a house or car) impossible, losing the professional licenses for which they went into debt in the first place (the ultimate, ironic bitch of a Catch-22), and even opening themselves up to being sued for their loan's value. Due to financial commitments to loan debt and under- and unemployment, fewer college grads can afford to (or, if they default, are completely unable to thanks to abysmal credit scores) make significant purchases like for homes or cars—the very purchases that incidentally are known to help aid economic recovery (Brown & Caldwell, 2013). And thus the cycle continues, perpetuating our horrible economy.

So basically we're all screwed on all levels, right?

I mean, kind of. But maybe not! Although I absolutely refuse to deny that this system is broken and horrible and desperately needs to be reformed, there are definitely ways to make informed, pragmatic decisions within the context of what is frankly a really bad situation.

Show me the money . . . options. However, despite this lovely picture I've painted, for many students there's just no way to get a college education without taking out a loan. But not to fear, there is a way to take out a loan without absolutely destroying your life. Having solid information goes a long way toward making smart decisions, so without further ado, here is the basic guide to your student loan options.

Federal student loans. Overall, a federal loan is the best option you have if you do have to take out loans and is *absolutely* the way to go over private loans (see next section). Keep these things in mind if you have the chance to get a federal loan:

◊ These loans are given directly to each school by the U.S. government on a year-by-year basis (therefore, the aid you're offered could change annually).

◊ Federal loans offer a single, low fixed interest rate (good) and flexible repayment options (awesome).

◊ There are special programs available for unemployed and/or low-income borrowers as well as programs for those who worked or work in public service.

For more information on all types of federal loans, visit the U.S. Department of Education's website: http://studentaid.ed.gov. Also check out tools like this loan calculator, which helps you estimate how big your loan payments will be and the type of salary you'll need to make those payments: http://www.finaid.org/calculators/loanpayments.phtml.

Private student loans. Private student loans are the devil. Seriously, if you take away one thing from this book please let it be this: *Private student loans are akin to Lord Voldemort*—they are best unspoken of and will hopefully one day be defeated by a boy with a lightning bolt scar.

Private student loans are provided by commercial banks and credit unions and are issued to students who have exhausted all other financial options and are still not able to handle the cost of college. Private loans have variable interest rates (which means they can change at any time while you still have the loan) and nonstandardized repayment schedules (which makes it harder to budget for paying off the loan).

Seriously, if you find yourself in a situation where you can only afford a certain college by taking out a private loan, you should seriously consider attending a different school. Being able to call yourself a Bobcat/Panther/Tiger/Other Exotic Cat is definitely not worth financial ruin.

It's also worth noting that although the common refrain about student loans is "student loan debt is good debt," that may not actually be the case. Financial prodigy Zac Bissonnette argues in his 2010 book *Debt Free U* that student debt is actually bad debt, because:

1. **It's an illiquid investment:** You can't directly cash in your education to pay off your loan debt. The only way to "cash in" your education is through the hopefully well-paying job the education allows you to get. You know, the type of jobs that are not exactly abundantly available these days and are only getting scarcer.

2. **It has a lack of residual value:** Residual value is the amount something is worth after you've invested in it. If the value of a college education to you is good employment, then it can hardly be said to hold its value over time. Because there's only cash flowing from your end with no promise of interest or a return on your investment, it's a crappy deal.

3. **There's full recourse and no collateral:** Full recourse means that no matter what happens (you lose your job, you become sick), you still can't get out of your debt. If you default, whoever issued you your loan can (and will) do *anything* to get their money back. Because there's no collateral (a protection against defaulting), the lender is allowed to go after personal assets or absolutely anything else.

Your Other Syllabus

Essential Books About Student Debt

***Debt Free U* by Zac Bissonnette:** Bissonnette—a personal finance expert—published this book while still a student at the University of Massachusetts, and his firsthand knowledge is a major advantage. *Debt Free U* chronicles both how Zac personally managed to graduate without crippling debt and how any other student can, too. This book is seriously all you need to make smart financial decisions about your college education.

***The Student Loan Scam: The Most Oppressive Debt in U.S. History and How We Can Fight Back* by Allan Collinge:** Collinge critically explores the $85-billion student loan industry, arguing that student loans are the most oppressive, profitable and monopolized debt in American history. *The Student Loan Scam* takes nonprofit and for-profit student loan companies as well as poor legislation to task for destructing the lives of countless students.

Obviously, this is all very basic, general information. Any decisions you make about taking out loans should be discussed with your parents, a banker, or any other financial advisor you trust. You should also do further research on the topic—I am certainly not an expert and am in no position to be giving definitive advice beyond presenting you with these facts.

But, because this is a guidebook and I am your self-appointed spiritual guide, I *do* have some tips and potential solutions. Thus, I present my *College Finance Tips for Smart Girls*.

Thoroughly research all of your options. This whole process is about education, right? Well, lucky for you that starts before you even set foot in a classroom. Do your homework: Don't get lazy with your scholarship search and take your time filing for financial aid. Those forms can be kind of tricky and convoluted but don't let a clerical error keep you from cash. For example, be aware that your family should file its taxes early the year you apply for college because no college will finalize a financial aid package until you or your parents (if you're dependent) file current tax forms. If you go the loan route, make sure you talk to *multiple* people about what option makes the most sense for your financial situation. Also, college price tags can be deceptive—use tools like college cost calculators (like CNN's: http://cgi.money.cnn.com/tools/collegecost/collegecost.html) to get a really thorough understanding of what kind of money you're talking about.

Ask for advice, but take it with a grain of salt. Although you definitely shouldn't devise your entire plan for paying for college alone (because, come on, rising freshmen are like a half step removed from childhood and this is a huge responsibility), you also need to be aware of the varying interests of those advising you. For example, high school guidance counselors probably want you to choose the most elite (i.e., expensive) college possible, and may steer you in that direction even if it doesn't financially make sense for you because it makes them look good. Admissions officers and other college representatives' jobs are to sell their college to you and will therefore likely make claims or stretch the truth about financial aid and other financial opportunities to get you to buy in. Collegiate financial aid officers will do what they can to help you cover tuition . . . but it's not their place (and it's not in their interest) to advise you that you really can't afford to go to their school in the first place. And then there are family and friends who likely do have your complete best interest at heart, but may not have the financial savvy to give you the help or advice you need. Your best bet is to do your own research, consider the advice offered by all of these people, but ultimately make your *own* decision.

Don't rule out public schools and even community college—at least for a couple years. If you're already preparing for your freshman year at a private college, this tip may be lost on you, and I certainly don't want to diss private schools (hell, I go to one). But from a strictly financial perspective, going to a public school (or, better yet, community college) is absolutely the best option in terms of avoiding debt (unless you're on a full ride or got some other kind of sweet deal—then by all means go enjoy your state-of-the-art student center and five-star-hotel-like dorms).

By definition, public colleges and universities are *publicly funded*, which means that state taxpayers contribute to the institution's costs. If you're looking at college like an investment, not just an experience (which you really should be), your ROI (return on investment) will likely be much higher at a public school because you'll have less debt working against your future earnings.

Also, although there is still a pretty pervasive stigma about attending community college from an academic and social perspective, financially it's your best option. Even attending community college for your first year or 2 to knock out prerequisite classes (which are essentially the same everywhere) is advantageous. It's also a well-kept secret that you

MYTHS ABOUT ELITE COLLEGES AND MAKING YOUR FORTUNE

There's a pretty pervasive conception that only graduates of elite schools end up making a ton of money. This is unequivocally untrue. Here are three myths that support that idea, busted:

1. **Your school's reputation matters in terms of postgraduate employment and income:** A 2000 study by Alan B. Krueger entitled "Students Smart Enough to Get Into Elite Schools May Not Need To Bother" found that there was no significant difference in later earnings between those who had gone to elite schools and those who had been accepted to them but went elsewhere (as cited in Bissonnette, 2010). So if a student is intelligent enough to get *into* an elite college, there's no real point in going into debt to go there—she is likely to make a similar salary (and have a better return on her investment) after attending a cheaper school than if she had spent tens of thousands of dollars more.

2. **Elite schools cost more because you'll eventually make more money after graduating from them:** In fact, studies have found that the amount a school spends on each student does have a fairly strong correlation with later earnings success. The thing is, though, *public research universities* spend more on instructional costs and their students than do private schools despite the significant difference in tuition (Bissonnette, 2010). It's also worth noting that of the nation's 2010 top 20 Fortune 500 CEOs, only 3 went to "elite" colleges (Bissonnette, 2010).

3. **If you want to go to a good grad school, you need to go to an elite college:** Don't convince yourself that attending an elite private college is the only way to pursue an elite graduate degree: In fact, 61% of new students at Harvard Law School received their BA at non-Ivy League schools (Bissonnette, 2010). Also, if you're thinking about attending grad school, it will be much more affordable if you spent less on your undergrad.

might be able to transfer to an even better school than you could originally have been admitted to by kicking ass at community college for a while. Many college admissions officers actually *recruit* transfers from high-performing community college students.

Seriously consider what you see yourself doing professionally and factor that into your plan. Yes, the world is your oyster and you have plenty of time to figure out what color your parachute is but then again, the economy never got that message. It's worth at least making a basic assessment of where you think you'll end up and what size payments you'll realistically be able to make toward your debt once you graduate. For example, if you know you want to be a teacher (or some other heroic and absolutely vital profession that is grossly undervalued in our society), you are in for a world of pain if you decide to attend an elite school that has offered you very little financial aid. But, then again, if I-banking is your calling . . . well, we have nothing in common but I wish you luck and will let you know it may actually make sense to go into debt for an Ivy League education since those are virtually the only schools elite investment banks recruit from and if all goes according to plan, you'll probably pay off your debt in a few years (for the reasonable price of thousands of dollars + your soul, but whatever).

Make smart daily choices while at college. We need to talk about credit cards. Here's the thing: They are not magic. I wish I did not feel the need to clarify that, but college students continuously get into credit card debt because they're not vigilant about curbing spending and paying off their balances. It doesn't help that banks target students for this very reason with student credit cards, which offer low credit limits, low-income requirements, and high interest rates, which equate to disaster. They are a trap and must be avoided at all costs. Getting a credit card is not a bad idea (if you can—they're ridiculously hard to come by since the economic crash) because, as it turns out, a super vital part of being an adult is having established (good) credit. If you do end up with a card, get one with a low limit and pay it off monthly like clockwork (now that you can auto-pay online, there's basically no excuse).

Also, make yourself a budget. At the risk of sounding like the Queen of the Funsuckers, do not leave anything to chance or spontaneity (unless you set aside some cash every month for the purpose of fun—yes, I'm advocating for planned spontaneity). FOMO (remember, parents, that's "Fear Of Missing Out") is a very real and serious disease running rampant among millennials and can be a serious financial drain. Deposit your monthly income into your savings account immediately and only allow yourself access to the money you allocated in your budget.

One place you shouldn't cut corners though (and the place college students usually do)? Food. I am not just saying this as someone who has had religious experiences with cheesecake, but from a health perspective. So many students rely on vending machines or ramen for their entire diet, but it's those crappy foods that can seriously impact your physical *and* mental health. I'm not advocating regular trips to five-star restaurants, but invest in some produce, at least: What's the point in spending a fortune on your education if your mind and body aren't well enough to take in any information or you're too sick to go to class?

Talking about debt is depressing, annoying, and boring. There's no way around that, and maybe that's why it's generally not something young women (or any college students) really talk about at length beyond a comment here or there lamenting how broke we all are and will be for some time. Maybe it's also because despite the fact that so many students are in debt, it's still a little bit taboo to disclose our less-than-billionaire status. But it's also a vitally important conversation that is the cornerstone of our current and future success and happiness—on a personal level and (at the risk of overreaching) for our gender.

Why do young women pursue college degrees? I go to a women's college so, believe me, I'm no stranger to being the butt of a joke about getting my MRS degree. And, sadly, I'm sure there are

LIFE HACKS

Student Loan Debt Edition

If you've taken out a ton of student loans it can seem pointless to pay them off on a dollar-by-dollar basis. Might as well spend that extra $10 on Chipotle and let your burrito work its therapeutic magic, right? But it turns out there are programs out there that allow you to pay down your student loans on a purchase-by-purchase basis effortlessly—and it adds up. Melissa Batai (2013) of Go Girl Finance (an awesome financial advice website geared toward women) revealed some companies that help you pay off your student debt—no strings attached.

1. **SmarterBucks** (http://www.smarterbucks.com): This free rewards program reduces how much money you owe and the interest you'll have to pay over the life of the loan by applying a percentage of every purchase you make on its online shopping market toward your student loan. The program also has an FDIC insured banking program called SmarterBank. Every time you use your (free) SmarterBank checking account, a percentage is applied toward your loans.

2. **Upromise** (http://www.upromise.com): If your loans are with Sallie Mae, Upromise allows you to earn a percentage of each purchase back every time you shop online through upcromise.com, eat at participating restaurants, or even every time you use a debit, credit, or grocery store card linked up with your Upromise account. Upromise savings can also be used by non-college students: savings are transferred to a savings account, 529 college savings plan, or even in the form of a check. So let parents, friends, and family know that it's never too early to start saving.

3. **SaveUp** (http://www.saveup.com): While SmarterBucks and Upromise provide rewards for spending money, SaveUp rewards you when you save it. SaveUp enters you into a lottery with prizes like cars, vacations, and even a $2 million jackpot every time you make a deposit in your savings account or make a student loan payment. They also provide educational tools to keep you up on your financial literacy.

4. **Student Loan Hero** (http://studentloanhero.com): This program is less a proactively beneficial rewards program than it is a really useful resource. Student Loan Hero simplifies loan management by allowing you to deal with all of your loans on a central dashboard (and advises whether or not loan consolidation makes sense for you), figure out reasonable repayment options, and design a plan that will help you save money and expedite paying off your debt.

some women who go through the college process merely because they feel they're supposed to, who are waiting for somebody to come along, support them and save them from the horrible fate of having to contribute to the workforce. But I feel confident stating that women with that "goal" are in the severe minority. Most young women go to college today because they're driven, because they are pursuing dreams and envision a bright future for themselves.

And most of our parents and other supportive forces in our lives encourage us for that reason. "You can do anything you set your mind to!" they tell us. "Just work hard, make good choices and believe in yourself!" But although those types of warm and fuzzy sentiments rooted mostly in faith are more than welcome (in fact, in the context of a culture that constantly objectifies, sexualizes, and demeans young women, we could always use more of them), they also don't tell the whole story.

Vague rhetoric about girl power and believing in ourselves fails to account for the hard, practical truth that we live in a capitalist society. Although women may define success differently than men—while we might consider healthy and solid relationships, a balance between work and home, etc. to mean success more so than a certain salary or a high-ranking position of power—the truth is, there is a pervasive financial reality to success, happiness, and even just a basic, good quality of life that can't be ignored.

It seems that many women are coming to the conclusion that they can only be truly happy if they are able to balance work and home—if they're able to pursue successful careers and professional goals and be present wives and mothers. And that's great, but achieving such a balance requires help. It requires daycare, for one thing, which costs money. Starting a family in the first place is ridiculously hard to do if you're in debt or if you've defaulted. At the end of the day, even being able to pursue what we feel will make us successful and happy requires financial stability, which stems from the decisions we make about college. And don't we go to college to be in a position to make those choices in the first place?

But beyond being able to create and account for the type of successful futures we want, we need to be more transparent about financial literacy as an entire gender. The second wave of the feminist movement derived empowerment from a practice called "consciousness raising." Groups of women would come together and discuss the problems they faced openly and honestly. In doing so, they realized that the issues they faced—everything from sexual violence to workplace discrimination to straight up dissatisfaction—were not personal failures but larger, systemic issues affecting *all* women. Once they realized that they weren't alone, they banded together and were unstoppably powerful. We need to do a similar thing surrounding student debt on a vast scale, but also need to do so as women facing financial autonomy.

It's actually ridiculous when you think about it: So many of us are in the same boat and could derive support, strength, straight information, and strategies from each other if we would only openly discuss finances and debt. I'm constantly astonished by how many young women I know who, although they have taken out loans, are barely educated about the types of loans they're saddled with and how those loans can and will impact them in the future. They seem unaware that taking out a loan can so seriously shape their future in the ways I've just laid out—and that there may have been other options. They don't realize that their financial decision could lead to delaying motherhood, could put undue strain on their romantic relationships, could sentence them to night after night of watching *60 Minutes* on their parents' couches into their 30s. Paying for college can potentially dictate one's life and yet so many young women either don't realize this or simply accept it as inevitable.

And to get a little hyperbolic for a second: *Especially* as women, we owe it to our mothers and grandmothers—who fought *so hard* for us to even have the opportunity to go to college, to pursue what makes us happy and secure our future autonomy—to take this opportunity seriously and to make smart choices.

Financial autonomy and responsibility is an issue we undoubtedly need to own as women on the greater level of pursuing equality and success for our gender, but at the end of the day, it is an intimately personal thing. Figuring out how you're going to pay for college is the first truly huge and impactful decision you will make as an adult and it's possible to make a smart decision that can lead to success and happiness. You are the *only* person who will answer for your debt. Feminist ideals aside, student loans and debt *necessitate* that you own being strong, independent, savvy, and confident in yourself. This is all on you, lady. But armed with comprehensive information, there's nothing stopping you from making financial choices that will set you up for a super successful and happy future.

CHAPTER 6

ANIMAL HOUSE, SMART GIRL STYLE
Your Social Life

When people talk about college, they generally don't tell the crazy story about the time they got an A in their Intro to Philosophy class. The go-to stories about (and general cultural conceptions of) college are usually related to its social aspects. It makes sense: College by definition is an academic institution, and is certainly a financial investment, but it's also a valuable opportunity to fully let loose, to meet lifelong friends, and stockpile great stories. Frankly, it's an opportunity for fun that, especially in the context of our severely overworked and overstressed society, shouldn't be passed up.

However, because it is such a distinctive experience, you'll soon learn that high school social norms largely do not apply. College is kind of like a meta sociological experiment: It's like boot camp for the real world (college students = adults in training), interspersed with a bunch of informal studies on human sexuality and the effects of alcohol on the brain. And, like most things in life, you'll likely find that your gender does make navigating these areas a unique endeavor, with specific rules to be aware of and serious pitfalls to avoid. But I have your back: Here's the essential guide to making the most of being social in college.

HOW GIRL WORLD CHANGES IN COLLEGE

Even if you managed to escape high school without feeling personally victimized by ~~Regina George~~ the designated queen bee of your high school, chances are if you are a teenager and you are female, you're well acquainted with the inane and somewhat horrifying social phenomenon that sociologists, psychologists, and anthropologists will be unraveling for decades to come called "Girl World."

Girl on girl crime, arguably one of the most rampant forms of crime that occurs in high school, consists of girls tearing each other

Your Other Syllabus

Books About Mean Girl Culture

It may be a little too late for these books to help you personally, but understanding girl-world culture is actually fascinating and reveals a *lot* about how women are generally raised and treated in this culture—and has really impactful implications for how women live the rest of their lives. If nothing else, deconstructing why that bitch Mandy somehow stained the back of your pants red and told everybody you got your period in sixth grade may save you some future money on therapy bills!

***Odd Girl Out* by Rachel Simmons:** *Odd Girl Out* thoughtfully examines the complicated world of female bullying, deconstructing everything from the way young women use technology to torment each other to how concepts like popularity and power play out, and provides strategies for how to put an end to the torture once and for all.

***Queen Bees and Wannabes: Helping Your Daughter Survive Cliques, Gossip, Boyfriends, and the New Realities of Girl World* by Rosalind Wiseman:** Wiseman takes on the dynamics of how girls socialize, analyzing girls' friendships, conflicts, and relationships with boys and their parents. Although somewhat directed at the parents of these young women, Wiseman comprehensively explores the elements that contribute to the social world of girls.

down verbally and emotionally (and sometimes physically, but usually the mind is the weapon of choice). There are plenty of experts who have intelligently deconstructed this world and the things that fuel it, and I will defer to them on this topic and encourage you to check out the sidebar for further resources. In the interest of moving on from high school and focusing on college (until we kick ass at life and go rub it in our peers' faces at our 10-year reunions, of course), it's important to note that socializing in high school as a girl is essentially based on power that manifests in the form of things like a struggle for popularity, the security (and wars) of cliques, and accessibility (or lack of accessibility) to social events.

But thankfully, college is different—and "different" here is the key word. There seems to be a widespread misconception that college is a judgment-free wonderland of self-exploration and mutual understanding. Although everybody does chill out (like, a lot), that's, unfortunately, not quite the case. I think that type of all-encompassing acceptance and love really only exists in isolated hippie communes—and even then there's probably some kind of drama about who is to blame for a disappointing hemp crop.

Bottom line: Even college students are human and humans need social structures. Popularity, cliques, and performing for others still exist. They just (thankfully) generally happen in a far more casual, low-pressure way and come from a place of positivity. Although the key word there is "generally"—socializing in college is hardly cut and dry. It varies from school to school and, like every other aspect of your college experience, is dependent on a ton of variables. Here are just a few factors that may impact your college social experience:

◇ **School size:** If your college is essentially a city unto itself then you're going to interact with your peers in a very different way than do students at a rural liberal arts school that has a student body of a couple thousand. It seems that generally, the bigger the school, the more free-wheeling you can be because people are hardly keeping track of you outside of your personal social network.

◇ **School location:** Schools often try to spin their locations into admissions pitches. *New York City is your backyard—there are so many professional and cultural opportunities!* NYU and Columbia admissions officers parrot over and over again. *This is a* real, authentic *college town—do your college experience right!* The University of Michigan insists about Ann Arbor. *Enjoy being sequestered by miles and miles of forest—what other school has a student body so diverse it includes feral squirrels and other woodland creatures?* Said probably no admissions tour guide at Bard ever.

But what they often leave out is that your school's location will inevitably impact your social life. If you do go to school in the middle of nowhere, chances are you'll be seeing the same people over and over again and will form a relatively tight-knit (and, on the downside, increasingly incestuous) community. If you're in a huge city, there are definitely uniquely urban obstacles that prevent a cohesive community, like the dispersion of students into the city to seek out "real" bars or cultural activities (not to mention the lack of actual, physical space available for parties). But then again, there's an endless supply of new people and experiences in huge, dynamic cities. Neither social experience is necessarily better—they're just very different and cater to different students.

◇ **School type:** Going to a women's college is going to radically impact your social life. Although a lot of skeptics tend to incredulously wonder how you'll *ever survive* without guys around, and it's undeniable that the sheer lack of testosterone is a pretty informative social factor, most women's college students don't necessarily view the absence of men as the major catastrophe that some assume it is. Sure, it's nice to have guys around as friends as well as romantic interests for those who are straight. But being in a community of women is also an empowering, comforting, and unique experience that simply can't be replicated elsewhere. And though I can't personally vouch for other types of specialized schools (like engineering schools or design/arts-based schools, for example) you can inevitably expect a somewhat different social experience at those schools, too.

And there are countless other factors that impact what being social will be like at your school. Every school is so different—the best way to get a good idea of what a specific school's social life will be like is to ask the students who go there. That being said, there are a few overarching myths about what being social in college is like generally. And, as per usual, I'm here to bust them.

MYTH 1
THERE ARE NO CLIQUES OR STEREOTYPICAL GROUPS IN COLLEGE—EVERYBODY IS FRIENDS WITH EVERYBODY ELSE

You probably won't encounter the type of high school mean girl cliques that have been popularized (and stereotyped) by the media. If you're in the band, for instance, it doesn't make you a "band geek" who just *can't* speak to the jocks. But the truth is people do tend to define themselves based on social groups.

However, although in high school these groups are generally all-encompassing, definitive, and even defensive, in college they usually emerge as a matter of practicality. These groups are composed of the people with whom you spend a lot of time (like the co-members of an extracurricular activity or the people on your hall) and therefore likely know the best. These groups aren't nefarious: Defining yourself in terms of group membership is essentially part of human nature, not to mention a perfectly acceptable and healthy way to bolster your identity.

These groups tend not to be rigid or exclusive, either. It's completely normal and even common for stragglers to enter or interact with the group—people frequently bring along friends they know in other capacities to certain group-based parties. Being part of such groups hardly dictates your entire social experience, either—you're totally welcome and even expected to have other groups of friends outside of your main or specialized (extracurricular) group.

So although depicting college as a love-fest in which everybody befriends everybody else is not terribly accurate, established groups do usually have fuzzy, welcoming boundaries. If you encounter a group that is more like an exclusive, catty high school clique, chances are they're just jerks and are the exception rather than the rule. Some people just suck no matter the greater social situation and you will find them everywhere. But one of the best aspects of college is the *overall* open-minded norm of acceptance.

MYTH 2
POPULARITY DOESN'T EXIST IN COLLEGE

Like cliques, popularity is generally a really aggressive phenomenon in high school. High school popularity is all about establishing a hierarchy of power and making some people feel subordinate and positioning some as clearly "better" than others. I personally never understood it or the complicated dynamics involved. I never grasped why some girls would rather be feared than loved, why they chose to take on what must have been an exhausting dedication to maintaining their status and calculating power plays. But then again, I am often told that I have an old, world-weary soul, so that might explain that.

Popularity does exist in college, but it comes from a much more positive place: It's usually unilaterally about certain really outgoing, funny, or just plain likeable people being well-known and respected, not about making other people feel bad or positioning them as "lesser." Also, unlike high school, anybody can be popular. "Jocks," "nerds," and "stoners" alike all have a shot at popularity, within their own groups and in the greater campus social scene. Because there is no single, power-based hierarchy, generally if you're a really cool person who has good relationships with a lot of other people, you meet a general standard for collegiate popularity.

MYTH 3

SOCIALIZING IS SUPER EASY IN COLLEGE—IT'S ONE BIG PARTY AND EVERYONE'S INVITED

Remember how in high school you (or at least somebody you knew) always complained about how you always hung out with the same people every weekend and always did the same things? You can't wait to get to college, you profess; in college there are a ton of different parties happening all the time, full of new and interesting people to meet. And that's definitely true—even at small schools there are always opportunities to go out and meet new people. But once you get to college, you might start to crave the kind of regularity that often dictates the high school social experience.

Although social things *are* constantly happening on campus and there are always people ready to go out and have a good time every night of the week, I'll reiterate that college isn't actually a love-fest in which everybody is included in everything—and that extends to partying. Just like you have to advocate for a great academic experience by constantly working on relationships with professors and staying on top of reading and assignments, you have to advocate for a great social experience by maintaining relationships

How Socializing in College Is Different

"Cliques and popularity exist, but in a different way than they do in high school. I'd say that cliques exist out of people's genuine fear of being away from home for the first time and adjusting to college. But where cliques were mean and exclusive in high school, college cliques come from a different place; they exist to provide comfort and support and, for the most part, are inclusive to any stragglers. I haven't experienced animosity or rivalry between groups of friends; people just tend to hang out with the same people. However people change friend-groups like underwear, and as people figure out where their interests lie and the kind of culture they want from college, their friends change."

—Aly, Barnard College

with a wide group of friends and staying on top of what's going on in other people's lives and on campus. It's up to you to get your butt out there—to keep up relationships, to find out what's going on—as well as make good choices about when, where, and with whom you should be socializing in the first place. Ultimately, it's not *hard* to have a great, active social life: A ton of social opportunities are out there waiting for you. But you *do* have to try and, beyond that, make smart decisions.

IT'S OUR PARTY WE CAN DO WHAT WE WANT . . . WITHIN REASON

I can't advocate partying in a guide to college for freshman women, primarily because that would technically be advocating illegal activity (which I WOULD NEVER DO) but also because my *mom* is going to read this, you guys. It might arouse some suspicion about the story I've been telling about my Saturday-night dates with Red Bull and a prime library seat. What I can suggest, though, is to educate yourself about what partying at college is like—how to have (responsible) fun, stay safe, and make good choices (looks like my maternal instincts are kicking in). And here's how.

TO DRINK OR NOT TO DRINK?

If you don't drink at a college party, there is a universal understanding that everybody will crowd around you and torment you. They'll shout horrible obscenities at you and voice your deepest insecurities for hours, until they eventually throw you into a pool/pile of garbage/whatever else is on hand. They will then douse you in Franzia, Natty Light, or another stereotypical college-geared alcoholic(ish) beverage available in large supply as a means of tormenting you about your decision.

Just kidding. If you don't want to drink, nobody cares. Basically, worst case scenario is you'll get some lighthearted crap about it for like 5 seconds—maybe a little longer if it's a guy who is trying to chat you up, and perhaps a little longer than that if he's already quite intoxicated—but that's it. There are plenty of reasons why people choose not to drink at college parties, and there are plenty of people who make that choice. In fact, about 20% of college students don't drink at all (Hanson, n.d.). And if anybody does have a problem with the fact that you're not drinking, rest assured that it's because they're insecure or self-conscious about their own drinking practices and want some kind of validation about it—and that's on them, not you.

But just a fair warning: Being a sober person at a party full of drunk people is *hardly* a good time. Although it's truly the best opportunity to observe humanity at its worst, unless you have a sober buddy by your side with whom you can make fun of everybody else, you may just want to explore totally sober social options (which can be great and definitely more intellectually stimulating). Then again, there's always the often thankless but necessary role of designated driver (or, in the city, designated walkers and/or cab hailers—yes, those are both things). No matter what path you choose, it's totally possible to be sober *and* social—and, really, just miss out on some regrettable decisions and horrible hangovers.

The fact remains, though: Drinking happens at college. Just like every other aspect of college, there will be many varied opportunities to consume alcohol and how you engage is up to you. But it's important to be aware of the reality that women approach drinking from a specific vantage point and are influenced by many factors that men may not be, including:

◊ **Body image issues:** Drunkorexia or "drinking without dining" is a female-dominated phenomenon in which young women starve themselves in order to avoid calories and to get drunker faster. This practice is often an extension of an eating disorder (i.e., cutting out food to compensate for consuming calorie-packed drinks) and, in fact, 40% of bulimics will abuse and/or be dependent on alcohol at some point in their lives (Dowsett Johnston, 2013). Drunkorexia causes short- and long-term cognitive problems (like difficulty concentrating, studying, and making decisions) as well as liver and blood pressure issues (Dowsett Johnston, 2013).

◊ **Sexual abuse:** Binge drinking is often a specific coping mechanism for traumas that disproportionately affect women: 20% of binge drinking can be traced to sexual abuse (which is one of the strongest predictors of late-onset drinking) and 50% can be attributed to sexual harassment (Dowsett Johnston, 2013).

◊ **Mental health issues:** Drinking is a widely employed coping mechanism for mental health issues—especially among college-aged women (and men). Redfield Jamison, professor of psychiatry at Johns Hopkins University School of Medicine, noted that college-aged students are at high risk of psychiatric illnesses but often go undiagnosed and, as a response, drink more, which, "undermines medications, can induce mixed states, make a person more impulsive—and put them at a higher risk for suicide" (Dowsett Johnston, 2013, p. 92).

For these reasons and more (like lack of self-esteem, specific peer pressure especially associated with sororities, the list goes on), college-aged women approach drinking in a different way than men. And yet, we're encouraged to approach it the same way: Enter bro culture, which is increasingly informing women's (and men's) drinking patterns in college and which encourages young women to be "one of the guys." It's actually the sexism of bro culture that often makes young women aware of the very real, yet subtle and usually unrecognized, sexist double standards that surround them on all levels.

"Bro culture" (also known as "frat culture") is basically defined by excessive drinking and its effect on campus culture is pervasive. Currently, about four out of five college students consume alcohol and half of all college students engage in binge drinking (National Institute on Alcohol Abuse and Alcoholism, 2013). An insane one out of every three college students meet the criteria for alcohol use disorder and hospitalizations for alcohol overdoses increased 25% for those aged 18–24 between 1999 and 2008 (Dowsett Johnston, 2013).

Admittedly, excessive drinking has always been a stereotypical cornerstone of the college experience (see *Animal House*, *National Lampoon*, etc.). But whereas it was previously never expected of and even looked down upon for women, female college students now actually *outpace* men in binge drinking on college campuses. A 2009 study found that female college students now drink 40% more often than they did in 1979, while the numbers for men didn't change (Kitchener, 2013). One in eight women now report binge drinking (drinking four or more drinks at a time; National Institute on Alcohol Abuse and Alcoholism, 2013).

This is our version of equality: Collegiate women are now expected to be both feminine and sexually attractive, as well as "one of the guys" who can drink and party as much as their male friends can. As *U.S. News and World Report* noted, binge drinking may have increased among women not because they have a gender-based alcohol problem, but because they are likely consuming drinks one for one with their male friends (Koebler, 2013). But in doing so, because female hormonal and metabolic differences decrease our tolerance for alcohol compared to men, women meet the standard of binge drinking far before their male counterparts (Centers for Disease Control and Prevention, 2013; Dowsett Johnston, 2013).

An August 2013 feature by Caroline Kitchener about Princeton's Tiger Inn Club in *The Atlantic* highlighted this phenomenon. The club, which Kitchener refers to as "the frattiest and hardest-drinking" of Princeton's eating clubs (or coed fraternities), increasingly attracts women—in fact, in 2012, more women applied to the club than men (Kitchener, 2013, para. 2). Girls endure things like swallowing live goldfish and being force-fed dog food while doing push-ups to secure a spot in the hardest partying club. Why? "They felt like gender roles were less rigid [there]," Kitchener reported. "It wasn't necessary for women to act 'all put-together'" (para. 10). One rising senior in the club told Kitchener, "'The guys always want us girls to chug a beer or take a shot, or be a man. There is no pressure for a girl to be a girl'" (Kitchener, 2013, para. 10).

This ethos, which is a growing norm on many college campuses, proves that not only are women not yet equal based on the discrimination and sexism we still experience in our daily lives, but because even when we do consider ourselves equal, it's an "equality" still dictated and determined by men's standards. To the women trying to make it into the Tiger Inn Club—and the countless women who sit in college bars across the country trying to fit in with guys by matching them drink for drink at their own peril due to an obvious biological disadvantage—conforming to the male social standard beats submitting to admittedly rigid female gender roles. Meeting in the middle—where women aren't scrutinized based on their ability to live up to ridiculous, virginal, puritanical "ladylike" standards, but aren't held to dangerous and stupid macho standards, either—is apparently not an option.

PARTY SAFETY TIPS

◆ *Always* **go out with and stick with friends:** The buddy system was not just designed as a way for frazzled preschool teachers to keep track of their students' tendencies to wander: It should be a nonnegotiable rule for going out. If you do choose to go out with people you don't know or if you're on a date with someone new, let a close friend or roommate know where you are and try to check in periodically. Better safe than sorry.

◆ **Watch your drunk friends like a hawk:** Nine out of 10 sexual assaults on college campuses involve alcohol (Dowsett Johnston, 2013). Being the victim of rape is *never* the victim's fault, but it's still important to watch out for your friends. Also, anybody intoxicated should never attempt to walk or drive home alone or go off with people they don't know. Do drunk friends a solid and make sure you stick together.

◆ **Know the signs of alcohol poisoning:** If your friend or anybody else you know starts to vomit, has seizures, is breathing really slowly (fewer than eight breathes per minute) or irregularly (10 seconds or more between breaths), or is displaying signs of mental confusion (if they're in a stupor or cannot be roused) or hypothermia (low body temperature, bluish or extremely pale skin color), then she probably has alcohol poisoning. These signs indicate that somebody has ingested a potentially fatal dose of alcohol and if you have any suspicions that she has, call 911 immediately. Seriously, even if you don't know this person, even if you're not 100% sure, and, yes, even if she is obviously under 21 and you're afraid that she could get in trouble—you could save a life and, believe me, she *will* ultimately thank you.

◆ **Be safe on campus:** Lock your door—always, as a general rule, but especially if there's a party in the general vicinity. Besides the fact that being woken up at 3 a.m. by some drunk random who thinks you're her roommate and who won't shut up about "that jerk Freddy" is a pain in the butt, it's just a good idea because she could be the least of your worries. Program campus safety's number into your phone and even put it on speed dial (if you're calling campus safety, you'll probably be too panicked to look the number up). Also, some campuses offer self-defense classes—it might seem like overkill, but while you'll hopefully never need those skills, you might be glad you have them.

However, even within this prevailing bro culture, it's possible to advocate for yourself and make your own (safe) choices. It's always possible to find parties that are a little tamer and aren't based on this type of behavior. If you do go to parties like this and feel others are peer pressuring you into drinking or doing anything else you're uncomfortable with, then *leave*: They clearly aren't people worth being around. If it's specifically guys who are pressuring you to drink, and if they're doing so in a way that leads you to believe they're trying to gain control over you, then the best option is to remove yourself from the environment immediately.

Basically: Drinking happens at college in ways both tame, dangerous, and everything in between. I will reiterate that drinking as a college freshman is illegal, but we all know it happens and that you will be presented with plenty of opportunities to drink and engage in other illegal activities. There is no prescription for how to deal with these situations: The only hard and fast rules I can offer (in addition to the party safety tips on the previous page) are that you should know and respect your limits, only do things with which you feel completely comfortable, and make sure there are people you know and trust with you and watching out for you at all times. As with most things in life, the best way to prepare for the unknown is to really, truly know yourself: If you do, you'll be able to handle anything thrown at you.

NETFLIX IS NOT AN EXTRACURRICULAR: HOW TO GET INVOLVED

Like I said before, nobody is going to drag you away from a *Breaking Bad* marathon and *demand* that you get off your lazy ass and join a club, group, or organization. Like everything else in college, your dedication, your involvement, basically your every action is totally on you.

Maybe after years of overachieving and résumé packing, of two-a-day sports practices, or a scarring experience with a truly deranged speech and debate coach, you just feel like you're done. You've put in your extracurricular time and, besides, what's even in it for you anymore? You *got* into school and have to wonder if a future employer in the field of financial consulting/advertising/graphic design is really going to care if you were the treasurer of the culinary society. What's the point?

But although the main point of extracurricular activities in high school may have been to demonstrate leadership ability, dedication, or specific skills to a college admissions officer (and, hopefully, was rewarding in some authentic way, but you know, who am I to presume such a thing?), getting involved in campus organizations serves a different purpose in college. It's something you need to do for *yourself.* Joining or even leading a club, becoming a part of a supportive group that encourages you to explore an untapped passion, skill, or ability, is about investing in your own personal fulfillment, development, and happiness. Whether it's a group based on academics, athletics, cultural interest, philanthropy, or beyond, extracurricular activities can actually be so much more than résumé builders: They can impact your life in authentic and rewarding ways. Skeptical? Well, here's how.

THEY PROMOTE LEADERSHIP

Despite my personal feeling that the most compelling reason to get involved in something is because you love it, not so that you can plot your way to world domination, access to a leadership opportunity is actually a really vital aspect of extracurricular involvement—and something, as women, we need to be vigilant about and continue to pursue.

The statistics are out there: Women are disgustingly underrepresented at the top levels of most major professional fields. Of the 2013 *Fortune* 500 CEO positions, only 4.2% were women (Catalyst, 2013a). Only 23% of all federal judgeships are held by women (Catalyst, 2013b). Women compose only 18.3% of the seats in the 113th U.S. Congress (Rutgers Center for American Women and Politics, 2013). And yet, studies show that companies that have a high rate of representation of women in management positions are more profitable and have higher employee productivity (Andersen, 2012).

There are a lot of opinions out there as to *why* women are underrepresented in leadership positions, including structural barriers (White men tend to hire and promote people that look and act just like them) and women's socialization (a fear of appearing too ambitious if we try to network or self-promote as well as work-life balance concerns that don't seem to affect or distract our male partners in the same way). But ultimately pursuing and having experience with leadership through extracurriculars as early on as high school and continuing through college will only better prepare us to successfully pursue leadership positions in the future.

THEY KEEP YOU OUT OF TROUBLE

Not to be a clueless, finger-wagging type who goes on about "kids these days," but extracurriculars really do keep "the youths" out of trouble. And although a lot of the research about the positive impact of extracurriculars is admittedly focused on middle and high school-aged girls, I think the findings still ring true for women in college. For instance, the U.S. government reported that participating in extra-academic activities leads to higher self-esteem among young women and enhanced respect among peers, which, they noted, can deter "antisocial" behavior (Massoni, 2011). The Girls Scouts specifically studied girls' participation in sports and found that the physical aspect as well as the team dynamic of sports reduced the likelihood that young women would make risky sexual choices (Kulig, Brener, & McManus, 2003).

Also, extracurriculars keep you from doing shady stuff because they cut down on your laying around time. I'm not saying you shouldn't have fun in college, shouldn't take a walk on the wild side (sorry, the old finger-wagger is back). But although letting loose is generally accepted and even encouraged, college isn't some kind of safe bubble free from real-world harm. If you experiment with drugs in college, you aren't immune from becoming dependent or addicted just because you're "young" and "having fun." Similarly, alcoholism is basically the norm at college, but nobody calls it that because it's just "college." Therefore, somebody who drinks an insane quantity on a daily basis, who feels like they can't make it through the day without a drink, is just considered an outgoing party girl—not somebody who is developing or has a serious problem. So many college students allow drinking and drug use to become their extracurricular activity and it's rarely questioned because it's so normalized. Getting involved in an actual, productive extracurricular activity could do a lot to save you from that really depressing fate.

THEY TEACH YOU ABOUT YOURSELF

Here's a secret about extracurriculars most kids aren't clued in on in high school: They don't have to be annoying time-suckers. In high school, I knew so many kids who would pick their involvement based on what other kids they knew were doing or the potential to bolster their college résumés. For example, they'd join the "Environmental Club" not because they were environmentalists, but because hardly anybody else was in it and they knew they could easily take on a role like "Vice President" that looked good on paper. Hence, our grandchildren will only hear about mythical creatures called "polar bears," but that's another matter entirely.

But, if done correctly, joining a group can actually be incredibly fulfilling and teach you valuable lessons about yourself and explore potential interests. I think our generation of women often struggles with taking risks: We tend to only get involved in things we know we can excel at and avoid new things because we're paralyzed by a fear of failure. But then, we end up leading much shallower, unfulfilled lives. I say we need to shed that fear and go after what we truly want, even if that means putting ourselves in a position of vulnerability, of accepting we might not be great at it. After all, nobody has ever learned anything valuable about herself or grown as a person by playing it safe.

THEY PROVIDE YOU WITH A NETWORK OF LIKE-MINDED PEERS AND A SENSE OF GROUP IDENTITY

Ask any current college students how they met their friends or significant other and more often than not, they'll tell you that they forged their most valued relationships through some sort of mutual nonacademic involvement. Getting involved in some formal activity or group is the best possible way to meet like-minded peers— and it's truly hard to quantify the many benefits of surrounding yourselves with people with whom you feel at home. You could meet someone who encourages you to take up some avocation you never thought you were good enough to pursue and end up being awesome at or somebody you connect with on a deeper level.

Basically, in high school, I found that I had two types of friends: Those with whom I had grown up, whom I had known forever and those whom I met through extracurriculars and with whom I shared values (like people I met through getting involved in a group that raised awareness about teen dating violence) or an identity (generally, social justice). It's the same type of thing in college: You have friends made based on location (usually, people from your freshman year dorm), with whom you bonded because they were nice, sure, but mostly because they were there and available. And then you have friends you made because you genuinely have something in common—a fellow aspiring journalist you met through the newspaper or somebody who shares your passion for social justice you met through your campus's Amnesty International chapter.

At the risk of generalizing, I've found that the friendships made from the latter source tend to transcend time and distance. It's those people that have pushed and shaped me in important and lasting ways. If I had never gotten involved in new things and joined different groups, I'd probably be a different person.

Especially at the beginning of the year, clubs and organizations will be in recruitment mode, breaking out everything from free candy to freewheeling compliments to entice you to join them. You have the advantage here: These groups need new members for obvious reasons (to replace graduating seniors, to reinvigorate the organization, to feast on nubile freshman blood, etc.). Take advantage of their recruiting impulse. Although these groups will certainly be ready to spoon-feed you an idealized pitch about their organization, make sure you get the real information—the time commitment, leadership opportunities, or other advantages (like internship opportunities).

THE TRUTH ABOUT GOING GREEK

In high school, I had a very specific idea about what Greek life was like. Informed by movies in which frat boys homoerotically got drunk together and then objectified women, and in which sorority girls were vapid, hierarchical bitches, I saw no room for myself within what frankly appeared to be an antiquated excuse for being a crappy human. I didn't feel any burning desire to find my long-lost nongenetic "sisters" or to participate in creepy rituals.

And yet . . . I found that living away from home for the first time in a giant city was challenging. I made good friends my first semester of freshman year, but we still hadn't bonded in that closer way: I didn't feel like they were shoulders to cry on or that I could have any kind of real talk with them. I craved the closeness I had with my high school best friends, who I really did consider to be my sisters. And for that reason, I tried to keep an open mind as I enrolled in formal recruitment at the beginning of my second semester.

It ended up being a great decision. Feeling like I belonged somewhere—among a diverse group of amazing and accomplished women, no less—was incredibly comforting. That being said, although 9 million college students are members of a Greek organization, it's definitely not for everybody (University of Missouri-Kansas City, 2013). It's a true commitment—in terms of time, energy, and (notoriously) money. But as somebody who in high school would've laughed in your face had you told me I'd one day be in a sorority and is now a proud member of one, I'll just say this: at least weigh the following pros and cons and keep an open mind.

THE PROS OF GREEK LIFE

♦ **The sense of community:** The downside of the overwhelming independence that's part and parcel of the college experience is how easy it is to get caught up in your routine and responsibilities and feel disconnected from something bigger. Being part of a very specific, inherently tight-knit group on campus really does give you a sense of belonging that being involved in a number of other various clubs just doesn't.

♦ **Easy and always available friendship:** Before I joined a sorority, the idea that dozens of girls would just be willing to be friends with me based on a common group membership alone seemed a little shallow and disingenuous. It wasn't until I actually experienced having a virtual stranger open her arms to me and accept the possibility of friendship without a second thought that I realized there was nothing fake about it—that actually, the world would be a much better place if we treated everybody like potential friends rather than a weirdo until proven worthy.

♦ **Philanthropy work:** A significant part of being in a sorority is raising money and holding events for and facilitating a partnership with a philanthropic organization. For example, my sorority, Alpha Chi Omega, is dedicated to raising awareness about domestic violence and has sponsored educational events for our campus and raised money for domestic violence charities. Nationally, Greek members form the largest network of volunteers in the U.S., volunteering an approximate 10 million hours each year (University of Missouri-Kansas City, 2013). We're all busy, but going Greek means committing to giving back in some way—and there's no downside to that.

♦ **Social opportunities:** Despite stereotypes, hardly anybody I know made the commitment to go Greek based on party opportunities alone. But, the fact remains: There's always an opportunity to be social when you're Greek. Whether it's a mixer with a fraternity, a sisterhood bonding event, or even just the ability to call up any of your sisters on a whim to hang out, being part of a sorority basically guarantees you'll never be alone on a Saturday night. Unless, of course a movie and a pint of ice cream are calling your name, but then again, there's always a sister more than willing to join you for that, too.

♦ **Academic standards:** All sororities require that you maintain a minimum GPA to remain in "good academic standing" (and therefore a part of the organization). If you're somebody who needs some kind of external push to keep your grades up, knowing that there are direct consequences for failing could be a genuinely good source of academic motivation. And it works: The national fraternity and sorority GPA is higher than the overall collegiate GPA (University of Missouri-Kansas City, 2013).

♦ **Networking:** Meeting an alumna of your sorority outside of your college's Greek system is actually an awesome experience: You immediately feel a bond and there's just an understanding that you will help each other out. This especially goes a long way when it comes to professional opportunities. Alumnae constantly reach out to their sorority at large as well as their specific chapters to offer internship or job opportunities and are always willing to hear from or help out a sister. Additionally, when it comes to your résumé, most employers understand the kind of responsibility and commitment holding a position within your Greek organization takes. They won't write you off for being in a sorority—they'll probably be impressed, especially if you took on a leadership role. And Greek members end up accomplishing some pretty amazing things: 85% of the Supreme Court justices have been fraternity or sorority members since 1910, 85% of the Fortune 500 key executives are fraternity or sorority members, and all but two presidents since 1825 have been fraternity members (University of Missouri-Kansas City, 2013).

♦ **Housing:** Depending on where you go to school, the availability of Greek housing could be a pretty big deal. At some of the bigger universities, these homes can be *really* nice and include things like personal chefs and other services. However, at others they're really not a big deal—it's pretty dependent on your specific chapter and university and also (I think) one of the least compelling reasons to make such a sizeable commitment.

THE CONS OF GOING GREEK

♦ **The financial commitment:** Yes, being in a sorority costs money. You have to pay dues, which can vary depending on which sorority you join as well as your specific chapter. However, most sororities have scholarship and other financial aid opportunities and are willing to work with girls who demonstrate financial need.

♦ **The time commitment:** Between recruitment, chapter (a mandatory weekly meeting for the entire sorority), committee meetings, social events, and other sorority gatherings, going Greek is no small time commitment. In fact, it can easily consume your entire life if you let it. Many girls actually like it for that very reason—they want to be consumed by something bigger than themselves, surrounded by their friends at all times. But if you do have other passions and commitments, it's definitely something to consider. You especially want to make sure you're leaving enough time for class and studying.

♦ **When it comes first (and shouldn't):** There are definitely sorority girls who take their Greek identity way too seriously. Whether it's forcing their sisters to stay up until 3 a.m. baking *all* of the cupcakes for some fundraiser, or just generally making themselves martyrs to the sorority experience, there are always going to be girls who didn't get the memo that Greek life isn't actually *real* life. Being part of a sorority should be a supplement to the other aspects of your life, especially your academic commitments. In fact, it's a serious red flag if you ever feel pressured by your sorority to skip class or not study as much as you should based on proving your "loyalty" to your sisters. That's *not* what Greek life is about and it's from those kinds of obsessive personalities that Greek life gets its stereotypical bad name.

♦ **Emphasis on partying:** Just like Greek life in general, partying should be a *supplement* to the rest of your Greek experience—not the center or defining aspect of it. There's nothing wrong with joining an organization for the sake of letting loose, for being social, and meeting new people. But if that goal becomes a nightly endeavor, if it begins to interfere with other more substantial aspects of your life and if you feel you're developing unhealthy habits because of it, then it's time to reevaluate.

♦ **Questionable social practices:** Although I do think there are some seriously unfair stereotypes about Greek life, there are some tiny nuggets of truth to some of them. The basic fact that being in a Greek organization necessitates the ranking and superficial judgment of other women is definitely nothing to sneeze at and is a really uncool aspect of the entire process. It's also pretty undisputed that legacies and girls of certain economic profiles are unfairly favored above those who don't have those kinds of privileges, which is, to be blunt, bullshit.

Also, a word on hazing: If it happens, run away. Seriously. Hazing is never okay and is actually a form of domestic violence, and yet since 1975, there has been at least one hazing-induced death per year across college campuses (Smith, 2012). I never understood how any organization could claim hazing was a form of "bonding" or why any victim of hazing could be expected to respect, let alone like, the person or people who hazed him or her. There are a lot of great aspects of sororities that are often misunderstood, but elitism/discrimination and hazing are downsides to the entire system that do actually happen, although by no means in every chapter of every sorority. However, it's important to remain vigilant and vow never to tolerate either if you ever encounter them.

ON CULTURAL AND MULTICULTURAL SORORITIES

An additional Greek life option is joining a cultural or multicultural sorority. Although sororities under the National Panhellenic Conference (the typical Greek life organization) obviously admit women from all socioeconomic backgrounds, they tend to be predominately Caucasian. Cultural sororities (which exclusively admit women of a specific culture) and multicultural sororities (which actively recruit women of diverse cultures) can be really attractive options for many women.

Having an opportunity to create cultural unity and escape tokenism by surrounding yourself with people who share your cultural identity is especially salient considering that studies show that elite colleges still have a huge diversity problem. In fact, a recent Georgetown study found that only 17% of growth at the 468 most selective colleges in the country has been due to the enrollment of African Americans and Hispanics, while White students account for 72% of that same growth (Carnevale & Strohl, 2013). Cultural and multicultural Greek organizations offer a great community for students who may be wary of the lack of diversity surrounding them at large. In fact, recent studies reveal that students of color do fear losing their cultural identity during the college experience. "[Students of color] feel tension between integrating into the dominant culture while honoring their own culture," Jake Simmons, author of one such study stated (as quoted in Byng, 2013, para. 14).

The National Pan-Hellenic Council, which was founded in 1930 and serves as a governing body for historically Black fraternities and sororities, is probably the most widely recognized (and historically established) of the many "cultural interest" organizations. Of the nine organizations the Council governs, four are sororities: Alpha Kappa Alpha, Delta Sigma Theta, Zeta Phi Beta, and Sigma Gamma Rho. However, there are also Asian American (under the National APIA Panhellenic Association), Latino (under

Out of the Mouths of ~~Babes~~ Current College Students

Greek Life

"I was the person in high school no one would have expected to go Greek. Even I am surprised I ended up involved since I'm kind of a loner, always had small groups of friends, and honestly, never cared about what anyone thought of me. I wore what I wanted, said whatever came to mind, and found my friends as a result. But yet, here I am in a nearly 200-year-old national society of 'sisters' and I love it. It's nice to be a part of something bigger than yourself. I feel good when I help our philanthropy, I feel content and somewhat amazed when I think about the fact that our rituals have been performed and continue to be performed for years by each and every member across the country. And though I admittedly sometimes take a step back and laugh at how superficial it can be to put tons of time and energy into winning a frat philanthropy or complain about staying up late to make baked goods for a charity event, I still feel empowered by doing those things. As a busy college student, it's my small way of making sure I'm doing something for others and it keeps me from going back into my natural loner-ish state. At the end of the day, it gives me something to be proud of."

—Marissa, University of Miami

the National Association of Latino Fraternal Organizations), and generally multicultural (under the National Multicultural Greek Council) sororities as well. There are even religious-based sororities, including Jewish, Muslim, and Christian organizations as well as groups based on other identities, like an LGBT orientation.

Basically, if you're at all interested in Greek life, a cultural or multicultural sorority may be the way to go. Beyond diversity, you could very well find that such a sorority exemplifies the type of leadership, character, and values (all qualities that should inform your decision to join any Greek organization) that specifically resonate best with you.

THE DIRTY ON DOING THE DIRTY: THE REAL DEAL ABOUT HOOKING UP

It happens like clockwork. It seems like every few months *The New York Times* or *The Atlantic* or some other major publication looks at their collective wristwatch and says: "*Looks like it's time to write about the fact that young women have sex for reasons other than reproduction!*" Yes, one of the many bullshit double standards young women have to deal with is the fact that while guys our age are expected and encouraged to have commitment-less sex, when women do it's literally national news.

THE TYPES OF GIRLS WHO HOOK UP, ACCORDING TO THE MEDIA

Adults are fascinated with the sex lives of college-aged women, as evidenced by such literary examinations of our behavior. But "hooking up" as it *actually* exists is far too messy, too individualized, and too personal to ever be summed up as a cultural trend and to be accurately captured by a middle-aged reporter. That hardly prevents journalists from trying to present women's sexual activity as breaking news rather than a series of often impulsive and nebulous choices. In fact, they've got it down to a formula, stereotyping women into several all-too-basic groups:

1. **The busy and ambitious girl:** Trend pieces like *The New York Times* story "Sex on Campus: She Can Play That Game Too" (Tayler, 2013) focus on the idea that hooking up is a necessary solution for women too busy to be in serious relationships. These women view casual sex and/or hooking up as a practical supplement to their true priority—career ambitions. "These women said they saw building their résumés, not finding boyfriends (never mind husbands), as their main job at Penn," the *NYT* story reported. "They envisioned their 20s as a period of unencumbered striving" (Taylor, 2013, para. 14). These pieces tend to focus on how commendable it is that women are pushing themselves so hard rather than question if the type of unbridled ambition that keeps you from actually developing a relationship with another human is healthy or even desirable.

2. **The female chauvinist pig:** Just like college girls are (to their own detriment) attempting to keep up with men's binge-drinking to fit in, they're also apparently trying to match their sexual standards by participating in meaningless hook ups and one-night stands. "Female chauvinist pigs"—a term coined by Ariel Levy (2005) in her book of the same name—are women who embody a male-designed caricature of female sexuality based on porn and pop culture at large. Basically, this culture is women saying, "Instead of fighting the fact that male-created stereotypes of female sexuality are objectifying—that you think I enjoy performing for you by acting like a stripper or perverted baby doll—I'll just fully own that persona and *call* it

empowerment." Back in 2011, *The Atlantic* threw their hat into the ring with its story, "The Hazards of Duke," which examined one student who created a list that ranked her sexual conquests (Flanagan, 2011).

3. **The technologically dependent:** It's a brave new world, such trend pieces argue, in which young adults can only communicate via machine, the effects of which even extend to the bedroom. Companies and apps dedicated to facilitating hook ups (like Grindr for gay men or Tinder for everybody) are growing in popularity and, of course, there's the way texting culture influences how "relationships" evolve over time. As one woman quoted in *The New York Times'* cautionary tale "The End of Courtship?" noted, ""Dating culture has evolved to a cycle of text messages, each one requiring the code-breaking skills of a cold war spy to interpret" (Williams, 2013, para. 3). Instead of dates, "Women in their 20s these days are lucky to get a last-minute text to tag along," reporter Alex Williams observed (2013, para. 4). These stories (somewhat miraculously, although not entirely accurately) shift the blame away from women and onto the digital age. Women aren't to blame for hook-up culture—it's the fact that an entire generation was raised to connect through weirdly abbreviated and/or misspelled phrases instead of full sentences and complete thoughts. How can we have a whole relationship if we can't even complete a sentence? Everything now is just so cas(ual).

THE TYPES OF GIRLS WHO HOOK UP IN REAL LIFE

The truth is there is no universal "trend" to hooking up: There are individual human beings with individual sex lives who make their own damn choices. Of course, there is some truth in each of the overarching stereotypes. Ambitious college-aged women often opt for a "friend with benefits" over a relationship. Technology plays a big role in facilitating a much more casual atmosphere for getting together and there are *certainly* young women who try to live up to guys' manic ideals of what women should be like sexually, informed by porn and pop culture, convincing themselves that that's sexual empowerment.

But none of these identities is a singular truth: None of them tell the whole story and most young women are still very much trying to figure out what we want, where we fall on the spectrum of these identities and choices. There is no *single* way women navigate their sex lives because there's no single type of woman—and women overall are still navigating our identities based on few existing models for how to achieve women-defined sexual empowerment and satisfaction. Billion dollar industries like porn are dedicated to shaping and promoting images and scenarios designed to satisfy men, but how often are we exposed to *authentic* female sexual satisfaction?

Rather than build our own definition of nonmonogamous sexual satisfaction, women are caught in a hook-up culture based on an impossible double standard: We can either be the prude—the aspiring mommy, hopeless romantic—or the slut and perform a male-dictated model of female sexuality. It doesn't help that the general conversation about women and sex focuses completely on women's behavior in such a dichotomous and accusatory way due to our culture's fear that women may want to exist independently from relationships with men, that women may even want relationships with each other (it's worth noting gay and/or queer women's sex lives are rarely if ever included in this conversation), and that women *do* have their own, unique definitions of sexuality (which society is hypersensitive about policing).

But one of the biggest (yet largely ignored) realities of women's sex lives is that far fewer college students are even having sex than we're all led to believe. Currently, only 32% of college students say they've had sex with more than one person in the previous year

(Garton, 2013). A 2013 study conducted by University of Portland sociology professor Martin A. Monto found that college students today are substantially *less* likely than past college students to have sex more than once a week (Parry, 2013). He blamed the perceived increase in students' sexual activity on the media's sensationalizing of hook-up culture, noting that between 2000 and 2006, hook-up culture was barely mentioned in scholarly articles, yet the term appeared in 84 articles between 2007 and 2013 (Parry, 2013).

Ultimately, college women are all just trying to make their own decisions and claim sexual empowerment within a context of stereotyped, male-defined female sexuality and a culture of double standards. There really aren't any hard and fast rules for how women approach sex today: Most of us are making it up as we go along, although I'm will-

Ask An Expert

Beware of Slut Bashing and Slut Shaming

To understand the aforementioned virgin-whore dichotomy in which women can either be "sluts" or "prudes" and not much else, it's important to break down exactly how and why women are shamed for being perceived as either. And who better to break down these concepts than Leora Tanenbaum, author of *Slut! Growing Up Female With a Bad Reputation*? In an interview, Leora explained that girls can be "slut bashed," "slut shamed," or "prude shamed." Slut bashing is a form of bullying that is "usually not even related to a young woman's sexual behavior . . . the term is used as a way to denigrate women and mark them as less than others." Slut shaming, on the other hand, "serves to police girls and young women to conform to the sexual double standard" and reflects how prevalent the concept of sluttiness is in our culture by allowing girls to "call each other sluts in person in multiple (often ambiguous) ways—as a backhanded acknowledgment of the way they judge their behavior, as a way to lightly tease each other, and even as a term of endearment." On the other end of the spectrum, women are "prude shamed" when they are perceived as someone who is "sexually ignorant, that you're not keeping up with your peers, that you're not 'normal.'"

It's important not to take these attitudes about "sluts" and "prudes" personally. If somebody engages in any of these behaviors, realize they're doing so based on their social conditioning and that it doesn't reflect your personal character. If anything, it's reflective of the person choosing to shame or bash somebody else.

ing to bet that the majority of college women actually want something in between a super-serious relationship and detached or even demeaning sex. Women are just a group of human beings (always a shocking revelation) trying to navigate one aspect of our lives the best way we know how.

My advice on hooking up? Do what makes you happy. It might take some experimentation and a variety of partners, some bad choices and hopefully many good ones, but you'll figure out what works best for you. And if anybody makes you feel bad about it, remember that some people are just small-minded haters and focus on yourself.

DO MILLENNIALS EVEN DATE ANYMORE?

If you do choose to believe the media that displays our generation as unilaterally opposed to monogamy, you may conclude that nobody in college dates or has a boyfriend or girlfriend. Surveys do tend to back up that idea: College students are less likely to have a regular sexual partner and are more likely to report that their sexual partners are friends or casual partners (Parry, 2013). Yet, of course, a quick scan of Facebook will show you that plenty of people are still in relationships. And it's not just those who have crazy stories about growing up with a person since infancy then falling in love and sharing a type of bond that transcends time, space, and distance and inspires novels and films. People who come to college single meet super special people, date them in a way that transcends a trip to Chipotle, and even enter into committed relationships. It's almost like we're all different people who want and pursue different things in our romantic lives. Weird.

Basically, if you want to date and/or be in a relationship, it's certainly possible. Hook-up culture may be pervasive, but that doesn't erase the fact that college is full of opportunities to meet fascinating new people—which seemingly should be a pretty conducive environment for burgeoning relationships. I can't give you a play-by-play for how to be the most alluring woman alive (that seems to be *Cosmopolitan*'s undisputed territory), but here are some tips about dating in college:

◊ **Beware of the "open relationship":** I know so many girls who have gotten halfway through a first date (or, in some cases even a second or third) before their date casually mentions that they're actually in a relationship with somebody. "Don't worry, it's an open relationship," they always say (like that's reassuring). I don't want to sound close-minded: Maybe open relationships, especially in long-distance situations, work for some couples and it's not impossible that some couples legitimately agree to try one out. But more often than not, it's a lame excuse for what's probably a straight-up attempt to cheat. And if that's the case, it's definitely not okay to pursue that person. Even if you do get confirmation that their significant other really is okay with sharing their boyfriend or girlfriend, you need to seriously ask yourself if *you* are, too.

◊ **Don't agree to keep hooking up if you really want a relationship or vice versa:** There is absolutely nothing wrong with a one night stand, with being in an open relationship, with being friends with benefits—whatever the situation is—if you're cool with it. If you're being safe, and you find it satisfying, I say go for it. But absolutely do not enter into any kind of arrangement with a goal not shared by your partner. You're inevitably setting yourself up for a lot of hurt feelings and disappointment. Even if you do end up getting what you want, like if you convince the person to enter a relationship even if he or she initially was only interested in hooking up, building a relationship based on forcing somebody else into a situation he or she isn't 100% on board with isn't always a great predictor of long-term success.

◊ **Certain people are just off limits:** College is definitely a time for sexual exploration, for hooking up with or dating people you aren't sure are your "type" and beyond. But there are limits for everything. For instance, especially if you don't have serious intentions, dating or hooking up with somebody you're bound to see all of the time—like somebody who lives on your hall, a lab partner, or another member of a really small extracurricular group—is just not a good idea. Of course, it's easy to throw caution to the wind, consequences be damned, when you're in the heat of the moment, but I promise dealing with the awkwardness or even straight-up passive aggression or hostility of somebody you see all of the time if things go badly (as they so often do) may not prove to be worth it.

Also, TAs, professors, and bosses: OFF LIMITS. It's a fantasy for a lot of women (that power and intelligence can be quite alluring), but it's never a good idea to cross the line of the formal teacher-student or boss-employee relationship and, depending on the situation, it could potentially get one or both of you in a lot of trouble (and, in the case of TAs and professors, if it doesn't actually violate some kind of school policy, it probably should).

TO BREAK UP OR NOT TO BREAK UP? THAT IS THE QUESTION

It's the question every high school couple faces when they prepare to head off to different schools: Should we try long distance? Although you and your significant other are (obviously) the only people who truly understand your relationship, you'll find that *everybody* will have an opinion about its future. It's likely that your parents and friends will be wary about the prospect of you staying with your high school sweetheart, especially if you're going to different schools and *especially* if those schools are geographically distant.

"Why would you want to hold yourself back by staying with somebody from high school?" you'll inevitably be asked. "College is a time for exploration—for new experiences with new people," somebody will probably pat themselves on the back for pointing out to you. And then there are the facts: Less than 2% of high school relationships will last past graduation and of the high school couples who actually do get married, half will end in divorce (Yates, 2009).

These are all valid points. In fact, there are *many* valid reasons to break up with your boyfriend or girlfriend when going off to college, including:

◊ **Physically holding yourself back:** Especially if you go to different schools, you might allocate free time you could've spent establishing your own life on your own campus by going to visit your significant other and getting to know his or her friends. There's nothing inherently wrong with this—you could certainly meet cool people at your boyfriend or girlfriend's school. But you deserve to have your own independent experience. You should embrace establishing your own life beyond your significant other's. And, in case of a break up, it's important to have a support system and other valuable people in your life. Letting your entire existence revolve around someone else is *never* a healthy choice.

◊ **Emotionally holding yourself back:** Establishing yourself at college your freshman year is difficult but necessary: It's the same process you'll undoubtedly have to repeat throughout your life every time you have a new job or move to a new city or even just make new friends. Especially if you're introverted or shy, it's all too easy to rely on an already established relationship during this time, to use it as a crutch and keep yourself from engaging in the difficult but vitally important process of connecting with new people. It's especially hard to grow as an individual if you're still trying to be the same person your significant other fell for in your teens. You owe it to yourself to find out everything you're capable of and the fully amazing person you can be.

◇ **Holding yourself back from other informative relationships:** One of the amazing things about college is that people with different life experiences and points of view sur-

Out of the Mouths of ~~Babes~~ Current College Students
Long-Distance Relationships

The Good: "I've been in a really good, healthy, and strong relationship since high school with a man who respects, cares, and loves me. He's supportive, wants the best for me always and believes that I can do anything I set my mind to. My sorority sisters give me a hard time about it because they think I should be having more fun and hooking up, but for me being in a relationship of 3 years is fun. I don't have to hide who I am and I'm always smiling and laughing because my boyfriend and I are on the same wavelength. Anything can happen in the future, but right now, I'm doing what feels right and what makes me happy."
—Hannah, University of Cincinnati

The Bad: "I started dating this guy at the beginning of my senior year of high school and we ended up dating throughout my freshman year of college. In retrospect, it held me back. I never exactly felt like I was missing out because I haven't been seriously interested in anybody at school, but I think it's important to feel independent during that first year. I felt guilty going to parties and hanging out with guys when I had a boyfriend.

"And it wasn't just on my end—even though this is *complete* bullshit—I would often make new male friends, who suddenly seemed far less interested in being friends with me when they found out I was in a relationship. While I wouldn't have been romantically interested in them no matter my relationship status, having a boyfriend definitely put up an unwanted barrier.

"It's also easy to get lonely when you never see your significant other and that can lead to bad decisions. It's better to just break up with your boyfriend or girlfriend (even if it sucks) than to continue to date them when you're not really into it anymore. You'll end up hurting him or her even more."
—Nora, Barnard College

round you. You may feel that you and your significant other belong together because you're so similar . . . overlooking what a relationship with somebody who is completely different from you could teach you. I'm not saying you should break up with your high school boyfriend or girlfriend in order to embark on a quest to find your *real* soul mate (although I guess that's a possibility), but rather to embrace exploration, to find out what you want and need from a relationship (and what you don't) by embracing the possibility of failed relationships with unlikely partners.

But, again, at the end of the day, only you can gauge what your relationship truly means to you and if staying together is the best option. I know it seems like the go-to, strong, independent lady advice is to break up and forge your own identity in the world. But as much as I obviously advocate for women being self-sufficient and truly believe no woman *needs* a partner, having a significant other can truly be a positive and empowering experience, and there's a lot to be said about sticking with a relationship with someone you really believe is good for you. If you do decide to stay in a high school relationship in college, however, there are some new things you have to be vigilant about that you may not have previously.

◊ **It's all about trust:** In order to maintain a healthy relationship while also establishing your own identity and life on your own campus, you need to establish boundaries with your significant other and then trust him or her. For your relationship to work, you need to trust that the girl your significant other is hugging in a recently posted Facebook photo is just a friend. You need to trust that they are telling the truth about their plans for the night, and refrain from texting them or their friends demanding to know their whereabouts (and, if you're on the receiving end of such behavior, put an end to it immediately). But beyond trusting your partner, you need to trust yourself. If you feel that you can't be around others without worrying about how it might look or, especially, how you feel about it, then that's a serious warning sign that your relationship may not be stable enough to survive long-distance.

◇ **Communication is key:** Although you definitely shouldn't be giving your partner a daily itinerary of your activities and checking in with him or her every 5 minutes (unhealthy behavior alert!) you should definitely be open and honest about what you're doing and who you're hanging out with. If you feel like you want to or need to hide something, like a new friendship, it's a serious red flag. And if you *do* meet somebody else that you have confusing (or pretty clear) romantic feelings for, don't hide it. It might seem like you're trying to hurt your partner by telling him or her you like somebody else, but actually you're doing the best thing for both of you by being honest and assessing where you're at before you *really* hurt him or her by cheating.

◇ **Check in with yourself:** You'll need to be incredibly open and honest with yourself about how you feel about your relationship in a way you probably didn't in high school. Accept that you and your significant other might grow apart and that things between you two will inevitably change due to a lack of time together and distance. There's nothing wrong with trying to make a relationship work if you think it's worth it, but also make sure you're not disillusioned about it. Being honest with yourself is usually deceptively harder than even being honest with your partner. It's easy to convince yourself that your only option is to stay with somebody who is so comfortable, who you have a history with, but it's important to stay true to yourself and open-minded about your options. Also, never, ever stay with somebody because you think nobody else will love you. That is untrue and a completely invalid, unfair, and unhealthy reason to stay in any relationship—long-distance or not.

I'LL BE THERE FOR YOU . . . IF YOU'RE THERE FOR ME, TOO: MAKING (AND LOSING) FRIENDS

MAKING NEW FRIENDS: HOW TO FIND YOUR NONROMANTIC SOUL MATE

In high school, I had five best friends who essentially were my entire social world: We did everything together and knew the intimate details of each other's lives. However, despite our insanely close bond, we have always been very different in terms of our interests and goals and always knew we'd probably all end up at different schools—and, alas, we did. Although I will always be thankful for the experience of having deep and true friendships during a time when girls often tear each other down, I think it was because of those incredibly real connections that I struggled to make friends my first few weeks of school.

I didn't necessarily have a problem meeting people: There was my new roommate, the many girls on my hall, and the countless students I met at the many orientation week activities. What I found so difficult was wading through the annoying (yet necessary) shallow conversations that constantly followed the same pattern: name, hometown, expected major, reason for choosing this school, etc. Even beyond my group of best friends, I went to the same tiny school my whole life, largely alongside the same people I had known since preschool. After almost exclusively socializing with people I had known since childhood, it was *beyond* frustrating to have to start from scratch. *Will I ever find anybody who I connect with and who understands me like my high school friends?* I wondered on a daily basis. It felt like such a basic question to ask, a concept better suited for a Very Special episode of Barney rather than a technical adult but I remember talking to my high school friends, wondering aloud: *Wait, how do people make new friends again?*

Ultimately, I was not fated for the life of a recluse—I did end up making friends. But those relationships didn't happen without effort, without constantly putting myself out there (despite my naturally introverted nature), and by pushing myself way past my comfort zone.

Of course, struggling the way I did is not the universal freshman experience. One of my best friends from high school immediately bonded with the girls on her hall in the first week of school. Another rushed a sorority fall semester and became completely integrated into that community. We all found our people one way or another eventually. There is no formula for making new friends, but there are a few steps you can take to ensure you'll at least meet new people with whom you'll hopefully bond.

◇ **Join extracurricular activities:** As mentioned in the section on extracurriculars, most people meet their best friends and the people with whom they most authentically connect through a group based on a shared interest or passion. Especially during your first semester, attend a few different groups' meetings to get a good sense of where you think you'll fit in and can be a valuable part of the group. Try to meet as many people as possible and don't be afraid to ask people if they want to meet up outside of the group. Get used to asking people out on platonic dates (it's especially necessary your first semester to do this).

◇ **Consider Greek life:** Greek life is based on the benefits of being part of a strong community. Once you're in a sorority, you can basically approach any other member and they will be friendly and completely open to getting to know you better. There are few other venues in life that are this amenable to creating friendships with a complete open mind. Even if you don't ultimately rush a sorority or feel like you want to drop out down the line, the recruitment process alone is a great way to meet a ton of new people—sisters and fellow potential new members alike.

◊ **Get to know your roommate/hallmates:** This is probably the easiest option. For at least the first few weeks of school, you should always keep your door open (except for when, you know, you need some alone time or are unconscious). It invites people to stop by and chat. Likewise, if somebody else has his or her door open, you should stop by and introduce yourself. Hopefully you'll also have a really enthusiastic and dedicated RA who does his or her best to facilitate hall activities that allow you to get to know everybody else a little better.

◊ **Be extroverted:** As an introvert, I know personally how hard it can be to put yourself out there and go out of your way to get to know complete strangers. But doing so is part and parcel of the freshman experience. If you're naturally extroverted, this is your time to shine. If you're shy, do your best impression of a person who has absolutely no qualms about approaching complete strangers. Believe me, if you don't overthink it, it totally works.

LOSING OLD FRIENDS: HOW HIGH SCHOOL FRIENDSHIPS CHANGE

It's an inevitable consequence of time and distance: Your friendships with high school friends who go to different schools *will* change. This doesn't have to mean losing those friendships altogether, but I'd be lying if I said it's not a possibility. It's generally a matter of practicality: You're imbedded in different cultures, surrounded by different people and other influential factors and will all change in ways that create an unprecedented gap. But there are ways to stay in touch and keep those friendships alive:

◊ **Set up a nonnegotiable time to talk every week:** College students are all constantly busy, but if you want to maintain a friendship, it's essential to keep in touch beyond a text here or Facebook post there. Skype and Google Hangout are livesavers—find a time every week (or at least on a regular basis) when you and your best friend or group of best friends can get together and see each others' faces and hear each others' voices and connect in a way that is facilitated but not defined or restricted by technology.

◇ **Make sure to actually catch them up on life events:** Even if you're dealing with complicated feelings or detailed situations specific to your group of college friends, fill your high school friends in. So many times during my freshman year, I would catch up with my high school friends and realize I had somehow just *not* told them about something pretty significant that had happened in my life. It made them feel like I had purposely kept something important from them, which probably made them doubt our bond. If you want to prevent your friendship from becoming superficial then you can't relegate your conversations and interactions to superficial topics; *really* keep your friends up to date when you do talk.

◇ **Cut them some slack:** Your friends are going to change throughout college. So will you. And neither of you can take it personally. Try not to judge them for any actions that seem out of character, but rather try to understand that they're dealing with new situations and new people and are trying to find their place in it all. If you're in a friendship for the long haul, you need to be willing to make it through some bumps in the road.

Being social in college may actually be as valuable an experience as any class you may take or content you may learn—but only in a balanced way. Partying every night isn't going to help you grow as a person, but testing your limits, making valuable and real connections with a diverse array of people, and tapping into new passions and talents offer one of the most meaningful experiences of growth you'll find in your (semi) adult life. It's these social experiences that will allow you to evolve the most as an individual and that will shape the adult you'll eventually become—not memorizing the process of mitosis or the intricate tenets of Karl Marx's view of production.

Out of the Mouths of ~~Babes~~ Current College Students

The Value of Being Social in College

"I have changed (for the better, I think) because of the experiences I've had from being associated with my school and a member of the university community. Being a student opened many nonacademic doors for me that have taught me more than classes ever have. I've learned more outside of the classroom, and a lot of that is attributed to the opportunities I've had to work with people on different things I wouldn't be exposed to otherwise. If I only took advantage of the academic experience, I think I would have had a very different college experience and I actually have no idea who I would be."

—Anjelica, Virginia Tech

So although the academic aspect of your college education is important for very predictable reasons—for the content you will learn, for the GPA you'll earn that will lead to graduate schools, and the degree that will lead to employment—the social aspect of college is equally as important for unpredictable reasons. It's the social aspects of college that will likely bring the big, blurry question mark of who you are and your purpose in life into focus, and that's definitely an experience you don't want to miss out on.

CHAPTER 7

HOW TO DO COLLEGE
(or Why All of This Matters)

There is no bullet-pointed list of How to Do College. There is no foolproof, detailed list of steps to take and things to accomplish before you graduate. We might perpetuate the idea that it's possible to have a "perfect" college experience that will transform you into an ideal version of yourself, superiorly prepared to face adulthood, but the truth is there are as many college experiences as there are humans who go to college: There is no perfect college experience—or any other type of experience for that matter (and I don't think anybody is ever prepared to face adulthood, but that's a whole other thing). At the end of the day, there are only individuals who have personal experiences based on how they choose to approach the novel situations with which they're presented. On levels both intimately singular and collective as women, we need to let go of this idealistic portrayal of college and embrace the far more nuanced and dynamic reality.

But accepting that this idealistic portrayal is false hardly necessitates accepting defeat: It's *more* than possible to have an incredible college experience. Sentimental and sappy though it may sound, you probably *will* meet lifelong friends with whom you'll make countless lasting memories. You'll attend classes and interact with professors who will change the way you view and experience the world around you. You'll get involved in a club or activity that will help you discover a dormant passion or ability. You will have a number of other life-altering experiences that I couldn't begin to guess at or describe.

Reading this book will give you a leg up toward achieving these things, it's true—I mean, where else can you find honest information about hooking up that doesn't present young women as one-dimensional caricatures, advice on how to avoid social leper status, and guidance on how to best navigate paying for school so as to avoid turning into a bitter conspiracy theorist who lives at home forever? But ultimately being a passive consumer of this information isn't going to cut it. There are still three major things you have to actually *do* in order to have a truly great college experience.

TO DO #1
DISCARD PERFECTION

Young women often view the college experience as another step in their quest for perfection. We enter with insurmountable expectations of having an idyllic, sister-like relationship with our roommate, of meeting a simultaneously intellectually stimulating yet romantic and compassionate partner, of finding an intellectual passion that will reveal a fulfilling life path. We envision a perfect experience because that's the standard to which young women are held to generally in this society: the prospect of anything less is a failure because there is no intermediary alternative. Thus even while immersed in a college experience that, as I've tried to describe, hardly matches this perfected vision, we don't assume that society has failed *us* in its unrealistic depiction of college, and that the college experience itself is actually much more complex than we expected. Rather, we conclude that *we* failed society in our personal inability to have the perfect college experience, that it's somehow our own fault. We struggle alone to create an experience that doesn't exist instead of banding together to embrace the one that does.

I wish I had a prescription to cure perfectionism. I wish I could draw up another nifty diagram or neat bullet point list to go along with all the rest in this book. But the truth is, I'm hardly one to preach about it—perfectionism dominated my high school career and hardly abated my freshman year of college. The deeply held conception that I had to be the *best* at any cost dictated every feeling I had about and action I took surrounding my mind, body, and worth. I ended my freshman year with a damn-near perfect transcript but as a shell of myself.

It was then that I had something of an epiphany. I saw the disconnect of passionately fighting for women to have access to the lives they want and yet personally feeling defeated and empty. I was reminded of the author and activist Courtney Martin's (2007) brilliant observation that we are a generation of young women who were told we could be anything and instead heard that we have to be everything. I had read and deeply related to those words years before, but it was only then, having stood on the edge of the perfectionist cliff, that I accepted their meaning. I not only fully realized that I *can't* be everything but also finally allowed myself to stop trying to be. I decided to exchange striving for perfection for striving for what I actually *wanted*—a distinction I previously hadn't even been aware existed. It took until the end of my freshman year of college to realize that striving for perfection didn't equate to happiness, but had only ever inspired the opposite and had robbed me of a potentially transformative year.

The truth is, though, realizing I had to change hardly made it easy to do so. Overcoming perfectionism isn't easy: It's about continuously making deliberate choices. It's about deciding to disregard the curse of the good girl, about purposefully ignoring what we should do, be, or look like. It's about deciding not to even try to have it all, but to try to have what we want and need. And to do that, we have to be willing to put it all on the line and embrace the risk of failure.

TO DO #2
WHOLE-HEARTEDLY EMBRACE RISK-TAKING

Numerous studies show that women are less likely than men to take risks, to go after what we want. This is not because women are biologically wired to be codependent rule-following minions. As researchers like Julie A. Nelson (2012) of Tufts University have found, countless compounding factors and different kinds of risk call into question the idea that women are biologically risk-averse. Rather, our general averseness to risk is historically situated and informed and, in my personal opinion, stringently tied to the perfectionism with which we're socialized.

Historically, women have only had access to autonomous decision making for a relatively miniscule period of time. As I've mentioned already, for centuries women were economically the property of their fathers and husbands, barred from making decisions about their own bodies and only obtained the right to vote relatively recently. But beyond the way this history of exclusion and subordination shapes the social, economic, and political context in which we're raised, perfectionism plays a crucial role in restricting our willingness to take risks. Taking risks means opening ourselves up to the possibility of something we've been taught to avoid at all costs: failure. Considering young women are socialized to view failure as the complete antithesis to our very identities, it's no wonder we're incredibly reluctant to risk experiencing it. Therefore we avoid risk altogether—we avoid the experiences and opportunities that could potentially inform us, and shape us into interesting, whole, and fulfilled human beings.

But, at the same time, college is an incredible opportunity to overcome this gender-specific ethos: It's probably the best chance we'll ever get to take the types of risks that will allow us to claim our own definitions of happiness and success and to finally go after them. In college, we have enough autonomy to thoughtfully and purposefully experiment—intellectually, emotionally, sexually, and beyond—but are still somewhat removed from having to make crucial, informative decisions that will directly impact the courses our lives will take. Now is the time to fearlessly figure out and pursue what we *really* want instead of going along with what we feel is expected of us. Only by taking control of our lives before we're inculcated by adult responsibilities do we have a shot in hell of the kind of happiness and satisfaction that can only be born from truly knowing ourselves and what we want.

This is certainly easier said than done, but we have to try—not only for own sakes, but also for the sake of all women.

TO DO #3
BE TRANSPARENT AND OPEN TO OTHERS

It's not enough to discard perfection and take risks: It's vital to be transparent about our decision to actively attempt both. Women need to be far more honest about the perfectionist pressures we feel—in terms of anything from academics, to the difficulty of finding and maintaining friendships and relationships, to the ways in which we treat our bodies and beyond. Collegiate women feel like they're struggling or failing largely because they buy into the façade *other* women enforce: that other women don't feel these pressures and that all failure—perceived or experienced—reflects who we *are* rather than something we've done.

Bottom line: We all feel defeated by life at some point or another, and we can break this cycle of internally struggling while externally projecting effortless success—which reinforces this perception of any struggle as a personal failure—by actively deciding to break it. We need to be completely upfront about the pressures we face and about what we're doing to combat them and acknowledge when we take risks in order to erase the stigma of failing. Being open about these experiences with other women will not only make them feel better or encourage them to do the same, but will cyclically help ourselves, too, by making this mentality the norm. By the same token, it's vital that we not only do this ourselves and encourage other women to do this, but that we're ready to accept them if and when they do.

College (and life) are challenging experiences. But they could be made so much easier if we confront them head on, together. Popular culture largely depicts college as an experience that leads to quantitative gains: as one in which an absurd number of parties are attended, friends are made, grades are earned, and a certain starting salary expected. But ultimately, the best college experiences are ones that are *qualitatively* successful. At the end of the day, college is a responsibility and an opportunity to put in motion the life you want. It's not about what you've tangibly gained but about who you are at the other end of it. I personally believe it's best to get an early start on achieving happiness for the rest of your life—you only get one of them after all. And a good rule of thumb is that happiness can't be counted or quantified: It can really only be felt and embodied.

The true beauty of college is that it's a period of your life that will truly be like nothing else you have experienced or will experience in the future. What all of the wistful adults in your life say is true: It goes by *so* fast. Embrace it and live every day of it to the fullest. Truly realize that even with this advice there's no perfect or ideal way to experience college, so just get out there and do it. Prepare for the highs and lows and soak it in.

And, remember, you're a smart girl. All you need is a little fearlessness, self-forgiveness, and acceptance (and caffeine and chocolate), and you'll be fine.

REFERENCES

American Association of University Women. (n.d.). *Know your rights: Campus sexual assault.* Retrieved from http://www.aauw.org/what-we-do/legal-resources/know-your-rights-on-campus/campus-sexual-assault/

Andersen, E. (2012, March 26). The results are in: Women are better leaders. *Forbes.* Retrieved from http://www.forbes.com/sites/erikaandersen/2012/03/26/the-results-are-in-women-are-better-leaders/

Baker, K. J. M. (2013). Yale officially declares 'nonconsensual sex' not that big of a deal. *Jezebel.* Retrieved from http://jezebel.com/yale-officially-declares-nonconsensual-sex-not-that-b-988475927

Batai, M. (2013). *5 programs to help you pay down student debt faster.* Retrieved from http://gogirlfinance.com/career/college-student/pay-down-your-student-loans-faster-with-these-5-programs/

Bennetts, L. (2007, March 31). The feminine mistake. *HuffPost Healthy Living.* Retrieved from http://www.huffingtonpost.com/leslie-bennetts/the-feminine-mistake_b_44690.html

Berkowitz, A. (1992). College men as perpetrators of acquaintance rape and sexual assault. *Journal of American College Health, 40,* 175–181.

Bissonnette, Z. (2010). *Debt-free U: How I paid for an outstanding college education without loans, scholarships, or mooching off my parents.* New York, NY: Portfolio/Penguin.

Blue, L. (2008, August 6). Why do women live longer than men? *TIME.* Retrieved from http://www.time.com/time/health/article/0,8599,1827162,00.html

Bolger, D. (n.d.). *Title IX: The basics.* Retrieved from http://knowyourix.org/title-ix/title-ix-the-basics

Bowling Green State University. (2013). *Marriage rate lowest in a century.* Retrieved from http://www.bgsu.edu/offices/mc/news/2013/news133952.html

Break the Cycle. (2011). *Love is not abuse: A dating violence and abuse prevention curriculum college edition.* Retrieved from https://www.breakthecycle.org/sites/default/files/pdf/lina-curriculum-college.pdf

Brinn, H., & List, Y. (n.d.). *The Clery Act in detail.* Retrieved from http://knowyourix.org/clery-act/the-clery-act-in-detail

Brodey, D. (2005, September 20). Blacks join the eating-disorder mainstream. *The New York Times.* Retrieved from http://www.nytimes.com/2005/09/20/health/psychology/20eat.html?pagewanted=all&_r=0

Brown, M., & Caldwell, S. (2013). *Young student loan borrowers retreat from housing and auto markets.* Retrieved from http://libertystreeteconomics.newyorkfed.org/2013/04/young-student-loan-borrowers-retreat-from-housing-and-auto-markets.html

Burnsed, B. (2010, November 19). 5 tips to avoid depression in college. *U.S. News & World Report.* Retrieved from http://www.usnews.com/education/articles/2010/11/19/5-tips-to-avoid-depression-in-college

Byng, R. (2013, August 1). College diversity still an issue at America's top schools, study finds. *The Huffington Post.* Retrieved from http://www.huffingtonpost.com/2013/07/31/college-diversity-issue-top-schools-study_n_3685145.html?utm_hp_ref=college&ir=College

Capuzzi Simon, C. (2012, November 2). Major decisions. *The New York Times.* Retrieved from http://www.nytimes.com/2012/11/04/education/edlife/choosing-one-college-major-out-of-hundreds.html?_r=0

Carnevale, A. P., & Strohl, J. (2013). *Separate and unequal: How higher education reinforces the intergenerational reproduction of White racial privilege.* Retrieved from http://www9.georgetown.edu/grad/gppi/hpi/cew/pdfs/Separate%26Unequal.FR.pdf

Catalyst. (2012). *Catalyst quick take: Sex discrimination and sexual harassment* [Data set]. Retrieved from http://www.catalyst.org/knowledge/sex-discrimination-and-sexual-harassment-0

Catalyst. (2013a). *Women CEOs of the Fortune 1000* [Data set]. Retrieved from http://www.catalyst.org/knowledge/women-ceos-fortune 1000

Catalyst. (2013b). *Women in law in the U.S.* [Data set]. Retrieved from: http://www.catalyst.org/knowledge/women law-us

Centers for Disease Control and Prevention. (2013). *Binge drinking is an under-recognized problem among women and girls* [Press release]. Retrieved from http://www.cdc.gov/media/releases/2013/p0108_binge_drinking.html

Dittmar, H., & Howard, S. (2004). Thin-ideal internalization and social comparison tendency as moderators of media models' impact on women's body-focused anxiety. *Journal of Social and Clinical Psychology, 23,* 768–791.

Dowsett Johnston, A. (2013). *Drink: The intimate relationship between women and alcohol.* New York, NY: HarperWave.

Ehley, B. (2013, June 11). 11 incredibly strange college majors. *The Week.* Retrieved from http://theweek.com/article/index/245398/11-incredibly-strange-college-majors

Ending Violence Association of British Columbia. (n.d.). *Be more than a bystander: What you can do to be more than a bystander.* Retrieved from http://www.endingviolence.org/node/1113

Epperson, S. (2013). *Student debt stalemate will hammer millions of undergrads.* Retrieved from http://www.cnbc.com/id/100850654

Fisher, B. S., Cullen, F. T., & Turner, M. G. (2000). *The sexual victimization of college women.* Washington, DC: U.S. Department of Justice, National Institute of Justice. Retrieved from https://www.ncjrs.gov/pdffiles1/nij/182369.pdf

Flanagan, C. (2011, January 4). The hazards of Duke. *The Atlantic.* Retrieved from http://www.theatlantic.com/magazine/archive/2011/01/the-hazards-of-duke/308328

Garton, C. (2013). *U chic: The college girl's guide to everything.* (3rd ed.). Naperville, IL: Sourcebooks.

Green, L. (n.d.). *Who is Laci Green?* [Web log post]. Retrieved from http://lacigreen.tv/about-sex/who-is-laci-green

Half of Us. (n.d.). *Depression.* Retrieved from http://www.halfofus.com/condition/depression

Hanson, D. (n.d.). *Most college students drink in moderation and many abstain from alcoholic beverages.* Retrieved from http://www2.potsdam.edu/hansondj/YouthIssues/20090828134831.html

"Help, I Am Gaining Weight in My 20s!" (2010, August 10). *Health Magazine.* Retrieved from http://www.health.com/health/article/0,,20429732,00.html

It's Your (Sex) Life. (n.d.). *The most common STDs.* Retrieved from http://www.itsyoursexlife.com/gyt/the-most-common-stds/

Izzo, P. (2013, May 18). Number of the week: Class of 2013, most indebted ever. *The Wall Street Journal.* Retrieved from http://blogs.wsj.com/economics/2013/05/18/number-of-the-week-class-of-2013-most-indebted-ever/

Jamrisko, M., & Kolet, I. (2012, August 15). *Cost of college degree in U.S. soars 12 fold: Chart of the day.* Retrieved from http://www.

bloomberg.com/news/2012-08-15/cost-of-college-degree-in-u-s-soars-12-fold-chart-of-the-day.html

Kitchener, C. (2013, August 1). 'There is no pressure for a girl to be a girl.' *The Atlantic*. Retrieved from http://www.theatlantic.com/sexes/archive/2013/08/there-is-no-pressure-for-a-girl-to-be-a-girl/278219

Kingkade, T. (2013, November 14). Amherst, Vanderbilt accused of botching sexual assault complaints. *HuffPost College*. Retrieved from http://www.huffingtonpost.com/2013/11/14/amherst-vanderbilt-sexual-assault_n_4271138.html

Koebler, J. (2013, May 17). Study: College women binge drink more often than men. *U.S. News and World Report*. Retrieved from http://www.usnews.com/news/articles/2013/05/17/study-college-women-binge-drink-more-often-than-men

Korn, M. (2011, January 4). Government sees high returns on defaulted student loans. *The Wall Street Journal*. Retrieved from http://online.wsj.com/article/SB10001424052748704723104576061953842079760.html

Krebs, C. P., Lindquist, C. H., Warner T. D., Fisher B. S., & Martin S. L. (2009). College women's experiences with physically forced, alcohol- or other drug-enabled, and drug-facilitated sexual assault before and since entering college. *Journal of American College Health, 57*, 639–647.

Kulig, K., Brener, N., & McManus, T. (2003). Sexual activity and substance use among adolescents by category of physical activity plus team sports participation. *Pediatrics and Adolescent Medicine, 157*, 905–912. Retrieved from http://www.ncbi.nlm.nih.gov/pubmed?term=12963597

Landsman, S. (2012). *What college tuition will look like in 18 years*. Retrieved from http://www.cnbc.com/id/47565202

Levy, A. (2005). *Female chauvinist pigs: Women and the rise of raunch culture*. New York, NY: Free Press.

Lisak, D., & Miller, P. M. (2002). Repeat rape and multiple offending among undetected rapists. *Violence and Victims, 17*, 73–84.

Retrieved from http://www.wcsap.org/sites/www.wcsap.org/files/uploads/webinars/SV%20on%20Campus/Repeat%20Rape.pdf

Love Is Respect. (2011). *43% of college women experience violence and abusive dating behaviors.* Retrieved from http://www.loveisrespect.org/43-percent-of-college-women-experience-violence-and-abusive-dating-behaviors

Lubin, G. (2013). A staggering look at the rise of college underemployment. *Business Insider.* Retrieved from http://www.businessinsider.com/rise-of-college-student-underemployment-2013-8

Malcolm, H. (2012, August 7). Women's financial power grows faster than savvy. *USA Today.* Retrieved from http://usatoday30.usatoday.com/money/perfi/basics/story/2012-08-16/womens-financial-literacy-confidence/57104200/1

Martin, C. E. (2007). *Perfect girls, starving daughters: The frightening new normalcy of hating your body.* New York, NY: Free Press.

Massoni, E. (2011). Positive effects of extra curricular activities on students. *ESSAI, 9,* Article 27. Retrieved from http://dc.cod.edu/essai/vol9/iss1/27

Mathews, J. (2003). *Harvard, schmarvard: Getting beyond the Ivy League to the college that is best for you.* Roseville, CA: Prima.

McLaren, L., & Kuh, D. (2004, May). Women's body dissatisfaction, social class, and social mobility. *Social Science & Medicine, 58,* 1575–1584. Retrieved from http://www.sciencedirect.com/science/article/pii/S0277953603002090

Moody, E. (2013, June 10). *When women couldn't get credit cards: 10 mind-blowing money milestones.* Retrieved from http://www.learnvest.com/2013/06/equal-pay-act-financial-milestones-for-women/?gallery=661&pid=#pid-7596_aint-0

Mukherjee, S. (2013, May 23). *Students allege four major universities violated federal sexual assault policy.* Retrieved from http://thinkprogress.org/health/2013/05/23/2055771/students-allege-four-major-universities-violated-federal-sexual-assault-policy/

National Association of Anorexia Nervosa and Associated Disorders. (2013). *Eating disorders statistics*. Retrieved from http://www.anad.org/get-information/about-eating-disorders/eating-disorders-statistics

National Institute on Alcohol Abuse and Alcoholism. (2013, July). *College drinking* [Data file]. Retrieved from http://pubs.niaaa.nih.gov/publications/CollegeFactSheet/CollegeFactSheet.pdf

National Institute on Alcohol Abuse and Alcoholism. (n.d.). *Alcohol calorie counter*. Retrieved from http://rethinkingdrinking.niaaa.nih.gov/toolsresources/caloriecalculator.asp

National Institute of Mental Health. (n.d.). *Depression and college students*. Retrieved from http://www.nimh.nih.gov/health/publications/depression-and-college-students/index.shtml

National Women's Law Center. (2013, June 10). *50 years and counting: The unfinished business of achieving fair pay*. Retrieved from http://www.nwlc.org/sites/default/files/pdfs/final_nwlc_equalpayexecutivesummary

Neal, M. (2012, May 10). Half of college grads can't find full time work, study shows. *New York Daily News*. Retrieved from http://www.nydailynews.com/2.1353/college-grads-find-full-time-work-study-shows-article-1.1075873

Nelson, J. A. (2012). *Are women really more risk-averse than men?* (Working Paper No. 12-05). Medford, MA: Tufts University, Global Development and Environment Institute. Retrieved from http://ase.tufts.edu/gdae/pubs/wp/12-05NelsonRiskAverse.pdf

Online Colleges. (2013). *A brief history of student debt in the United States*. Retrieved from http://www.onlinecolleges.net/2013/06/27/student-debt-in-the-u-s-part-2-a-brief-history-of-student-debt-in-the-united-states/

Parry, M. (2013, August 13). Study casts skeptical light on campus 'hookup culture.' *The Chronicle of Higher Education*.

Retrieved from http://chronicle.com/blogs/percolator/study-casts-skeptical-light-on-campus-hookup-culture/33389

Pew Research Center. (2012). *The lost decade of the middle class.* Retrieved from http://www.pewsocialtrends.org/2012/08/22/the-lost-decade-of-the-middle-class

Planned Parenthood. (2013). *Masturbation.* Retrieved from http://www.plannedparenthood.org/health-topics/sex-101/masturbation-23901.htm

Rampell, C. (2009, December 7). Money fights predict divorce rates. *The New York Times.* Retrieved from http://economix.blogs.nytimes.com/2009/12/07/money-fights-predict-divorce-rates/

Rampell, C. (2013, February 19). It takes a B.A. to find a job as a file clerk. *The New York Times.* Retrieved from http://www.nytimes.com/2013/02/20/business/college-degree-required-by-increasing-number-of-companies.html?pagewanted=all

Rape, Abuse and Incest National Network. (2009a). *Rape.* Retrieved from http://www.rainn.org/get-information/types-of-sexual-assault/definition-of-rape

Rape, Abuse and Incest National Network. (2009b). *Reporting rates.* Retrieved from http://www.rainn.org/get-information/statistics/reporting-rates

Rape, Abuse and Incest National Network. (2009c). *Sexual assault.* Retrieved from http://www.rainn.org/get-information/types-of-sexual-assault/sexual-assault

Rowe-Finkbeiner, K. (2004). *The F word: Feminism in jeopardy.* Berkley, CA: Seal Press.

Rutgers Center for American Women and Politics. (2013). *Women in the U.S. Congress 2013* [Fact sheet]. Retrieved from http://www.cawp.rutgers.edu/fast_facts/levels_of_office/documents/cong.pdf

Sampson, R. (2002). *Acquaintance rape of college students* (Guide No. 17). Washington, DC: U.S. Department of Justice, Office of Community Oriented Policing Services. Retrieved from http://www.cops.usdoj.gov/pdf/e03021472.pdf

Segal, J., & Smith, M. (2013). *Eating disorder treatment and recovery*. Retrieved from http://www.helpguide.org/mental/eating_disorder_treatment.htm

Simmons, R. (2009). *The curse of the good girl: Raising authentic girls with courage and confidence.* New York, NY: Penguin.

Smith, T. (2012, February 5). *Seeking an end to hazing deaths.* Retrieved from http://www.cbsnews.com/2102-3445_162-57371657.html

Taibbi, M. (2013, August 15). Ripping off young America: The college loan scandal. *Rolling Stone.* Retrieved from http://www.rollingstone.com/politics/news/ripping-off-young-america-the-college-loan-scandal-20130815

Tascarella, P. (2005, January 17). What women want. *Pittsburgh Business Times.* Retrieved from http://www.bizjournals.com/pittsburgh/stories/2005/01/17/focus2.html?page=2

Tayler, K. (2013, July 12). Sex on campus: She can play that game, too. *The New York Times.* Retrieved from http://www.nytimes.com/2013/07/14/fashion/sex-on-campus-she-can-play-that-game-too.html?pagewanted=all&_r=2&%29.&

Tysiac, K. (2012, May 4). Financial matters are top cause of couples' spats, survey shows. *Journal of Accountancy.* Retrieved from http://www.journalofaccountancy.com/News/20125634

University of Missouri-Kansas City. (2013). *Fraternity & sorority affairs: National statistics* [Fact sheet]. Retrieved from http://www.umkc.edu/getinvolved/fsa-national-statistics.asp

U.S. Department of Justice, Office of Violence Against Women. (2009). Stalking fact sheet. Washington, DC: Author. Retrieved from http://www.victimsofcrime.org/docs/src/stalking-fact-sheet_english.pdf

Wang, W., Parker, K., & Taylor, P. (2013). Breadwinner moms. *Pew Social & Demographic Trends.* Retrieved from http://www.pewsocialtrends.org/2013/05/29/breadwinner-moms/

Williams, A. (2013, January 11). The end of courtship? *The New York Times.* Retrieved from http://www.nytimes.com/2013/01/13/

fashion/the-end-of-courtship.html?adxnnl=1&pagewanted=all
&adxnnlx=1379433782-Jvmy3FbUIqB/kZM/*cD99lg*

Yates, R. (2009). Divorce rates fall as couples marry later. *The Morning Call*. Retrieved from http://articles.mcall.com/2009-06-28/news/4397779_1_fewer-divorces-marriage-couples

Zagorsky, J. L., & Smith, P. K. (2011). The freshman 15: A critical time for obesity intervention or media myth? *Social Science Quarterly, 92,* 1389–1407.

ABOUT THE AUTHOR

Julie Zeilinger is originally from Pepper Pike, OH, and is a member of the Barnard College Class of 2015. Julie is the founder and editor of The FBomb (http://www.thefbomb.org), a feminist blog and community for teens and young adults who care about their rights and want to be heard. Julie has been named one of *Newsweek's* "150 Women Who Shake The World," one of the "Fight most influential bloggers under 21" by *Women's Day* Magazine, one of *More* Magazine's "New Feminists You Need To Know," and one of *The Times* of London's "40 Bloggers Who Really Count." Her writing has been published on the *Huffington Post, Forbes,* and CNN amongst other publications. She is also the author of *A Little F'd Up: Why Feminism Is Not a Dirty Word* (2012). For more information, visit http://www.juliezeilinger.com or follow her on Twitter @juliezeilinger.